Out of E:

developing youth work
with young refugees

Ros Norton and Brian Cohen

with assistance from

Asher Eisen and Yvonne Field

and interviewers:

Mulugete Abraha, Xhevat Ademi, Sahra Ali,
Melanie Johnson, Hirut Kahesay, Fazil Kawani and
Andy Khalfi

Commissioned by
The Barbara Melunsky Fund in partnership with
Westminster Diocese Refugee Service and the
Evelyn Oldfield Unit

Published by
YOUTH • WORK • PRESS

*supporting and improving work
with young people*

YOUTH • WORK • PRESS is a publishing imprint of the
National Youth Agency
17–23 Albion Street,
Leicester
LE1 6GD
Tel: 0116.285.3700.
Fax: 0116.285.3777.
E-mail: nya@nya.org.uk
Website: http://www.nya.org.uk

ISBN 0 86155 241 5
Price £8.50

© November 2000

CONTENTS

Preface

Young refugees in the UK face immense problems of racism, unemployment and alienation. Many want to integrate with dignity into British culture and society while at the same time being free to value and cherish their own particular culture and identity. They also seek to be economically independent and to contribute to the economic life of their adopted country. But all too often they are hampered by language difficulties, discrimination and the lack of appropriate skills, training and services.

Since its establishment in 1996 the Barbara Melunsky Fund has been encouraging fresh thinking to improve training and education for young refugees. Its vision has been one of cooperation and empowerment. *Out of Exile*, commissioned from Goldsmiths Centre for Public and Voluntary Sector Development (PVSD), grows out of this vision. I wish to thank Goldsmiths PVSD for its hard work and commitment researching and compiling the report. My thanks also to my dedicated colleagues on the Fund's Management Committee who worked in close cooperation with the authors in developing the report from its earliest stages.

Out of Exile is a serious contribution and a challenge to policy-makers in government departments, local authorities, youth work services, refugee community organisations and refugee agencies. As discussed in Section Four, it is particularly relevant since the introduction of dispersal of asylum seekers across many parts of the country during this last year. It should stimulate discussion and, more importantly, raise serious questions about policy direction for all decision makers who are rightly concerned with the negative aspects of young people's hopelessness, isolation and alienation, now and in the future. I expect that the report will become a working document, forming the basis for a comprehensive review of existing youth work provision in terms of policy direction, resources and priorities.

In compiling this report the Fund and Goldsmiths PVSD are proud of the unique collaborative working relationships established between voluntary refugee organisations, academic institutions, professional bodies and young refugees themselves. I would wish that the follow-up debate and the implementation of any recommendations arising from this report will be carried out in the same spirit of cooperation.

Michael F. Feeney
Chair, Barbara Melunsky Fund (1996 – June 2000)

Acknowledgments

Our thanks must first go to those funders who have demonstrated faith in young refugees by backing this research. We are grateful to the City Parochial Foundation, Comic Relief, London Boroughs Grants, Reuters and the Worshipful Company of Weavers.

The writing of this report would not have been possible without the help, support and advice of many people.

We wish to acknowledge the invaluable contributions of our colleagues at Goldsmiths. Asher Eisen and Yvonne Field, both played key roles in the planning and execution of this research. We have been encouraged by the support of Betty Evans-Jacas throughout the research. Most important of all has been the support and patience of Selina O'Dwyer who has acted as secretary for the study and kept track of the whole progress of the research.

We were extremely fortunate to obtain the services of a dedicated team of interviewers who contributed much of their experience, personal and professional, as well as carrying out the task of interviewing. We wish to thank Mulugete Abraha, Xhevat Ademi, Sahra Ali, Melanie Johnson, Hirut Kahesay, Fazil Kawani and Andy Khalfi.

Many people gave generously of their time and their considerable knowledge. We would particularly like to thank Anba Ali, Mohamoud Aden, Said Behi Addiad, Radia Ahmed, Sami Aziz, Yohannes Asmelash, Lizette Gonzalez, Wafa Hussein, Diana and Misak Ohanian, Viviana Roesenkranz, Adnan Shaswan, Swaminathur Thangarajah, Selvany Thiagamoorthy and Zarina Vidale.

At different times during the research, Barbara Cohen, Charles Woodd and Elizabeth Mestheneos gave important and very helpful advice. Elizabeth Block (EJB Communications) undertook the final sub-editing with skill and helped us to meet our final deadline.

A very special vote of thanks is due to the Barbara Melunsky Fund and its two partner organisations, the Evelyn Oldfield Unit and Westminster Diocese Refugee Service which identified the need for research. Much of the impetus for this research came from Michael Feeney, Chair of the Barbara Melunsky Fund until June 2000. For personal reasons, Michael was unable to continue with his commitment to the study. Tzeggai Yohannes, who was a joint initiator of the research, took over as Chair and has been a pillar of strength and has generously given of his time in long discussions with us. Paul Buddery, Maria Kozlowski and Tesfai Berhane have made many contributions and given much support to the research.

Bernard Melunsky has given us whole-hearted support and advice throughout. His dedication to this work has sustained us all. The Fund is named after his late wife and it was a pleasure to meet refugee workers in the course of the research who remembered her and her work. As one refugee worker said of Barbara, she had always been a great support to his community organisation – she was always the first port of call in time of need.

Many people have helped us in this study but any faults in the study are ours alone. Finally, appreciation for the continued inspiration given by the young people in our lives cannot go unmentioned: Brian wishes to thank his daughter Rachel who read and commented critically on the draft and his daughter Hilary who kept his feet firmly on the ground throughout. Rhiannon and Katherine, Lawrence and Liam were always in Ros's consciousness – where would she be without you?

Ros Norton and Brian Cohen
November 2000

About the Partners

The Barbara Melunsky Fund

The Barbara Melunsky Fund was formed after the death of Barbara Melunsky, aged 49, in 1995. Barbara was Principal Grants Officer at the London Boroughs Grants Unit at the time of her death, and had worked for the United Nations High Commissioner for Refugees during the Indo-Chinese refugee crisis of the late 1970s and then for the Refugee Council in Britain.

The Barbara Melunsky Fund has funded training courses for refugees in youth work at Goldsmiths College and counselling at Birkbeck College.

The Evelyn Oldfield Unit

The Evelyn Oldfield Unit was established after the death of Evelyn Oldfield in 1992. Evelyn was one of the first field officers of the City Parochial Foundation and the Trust for London. She had devoted her energies to developing a strong and effective voluntary sector in which refugee community organisations played a key part.

The Evelyn Oldfield Unit was set up to provide professional support and training for established refugee groups and the communities they serve. The advice, training and support offered is guided by the needs of the groups themselves, which make up a majority of its management committee.

Westminster Diocese Refugee Service

Westminster Diocese Refugee Service is a Catholic agency that has been addressing the needs of asylum seekers within the Westminster Diocese and across London since 1989. It plays a key role in improving and coordinating policy, practice and provision for refugees, working with varied partners to do so. It initiated and runs the Inter-Faith Refugee Network, services and supports the Refugee Working Party and manages and administers the Barbara Melunsky Fund.

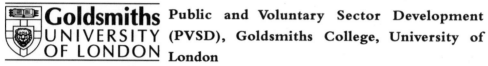

Public and Voluntary Sector Development (PVSD), Goldsmiths College, University of London

PVSD was established in the mid-90s within the Professional and Community Education programme area of Goldsmiths College. It aims to enable managers and practitioners to bridge the gap between theory and practice through learning the skills of critical reflection underpinned by the values of diversity and equality. A range of pre and post qualifying courses are developed and accredited, involving managers and practitioners of diverse cultural backgrounds across the public, voluntary and community sectors and in the fields of youth, community and social work, housing and health. PVSD's programme currently includes project development and evaluation; action learning; research; consultancy; and tailored delivery of training for organisations.

About the Authors

Ros Norton has been the Coordinator for the Public and Voluntary Sector Development programme area at Goldsmiths College since 1992. Since qualifying in community and youth work at Goldsmiths in 1979 she has worked as a community and youth worker, youth officer, supervisor, consultant, trainer and researcher in and for the youth work field. Her deepening involvement in the refugee community sector and refugee youth work has developed over the last eight years at Goldsmiths through sustained contact with refugee colleagues from all over the world.

Brian Cohen has been a freelance trainer/researcher/consultant since 1991. He was a tutor in Community and Youth Work at Goldsmiths College, University of London, between 1971 and 1991. Over many years he has sustained his involvement with youth work, the community sector and the refugee community sector. Among his recent roles, he acted as coordinator for the Community Sector Coalition. He has published articles and contributed chapters to books on race relations and social policy, community work, adult education and youth work.

Foreword

This report shows what is needed for young asylum seekers and refugees to stand some chance of reaching their full potential in this country. It shows the impact of being forced to flee one's own country at a young age, the struggle with a new culture and with racism. It shows the importance of support to parents who are also trying to put their lives back together while protecting their children.

The report sets out for policy-makers and service providers what needs to be done. It shows the costs we pay by neglecting young people. Support now will help children become confident adults able to contribute effectively to their new home. At a time of unprecedented hostility to asylum seekers this research is an important and welcome practical study. Its recommendations deserve the attention of all those who work with young people in this country.

Kate Allen
Director, Amnesty International;
former Deputy Chief Executive, The Refugee Council

Purpose of Research

In 1997, the Barbara Melunsky Fund (BMF), in partnership with the Evelyn Oldfield Unit and the Westminster Diocese Refugee Service, commissioned the Goldsmiths College Centre for Public and Voluntary Sector Development (PVSD) to offer a tailored delivery of the Goldsmiths College Certificate of Professional Practice in Youth Work. The result was a new part-time course, offered over a one-year period, aimed at developing youth work knowledge and skills for adult refugees working with young people in refugee community organisations. Much was learned from that programme and a separate evaluation report was produced. This report highlighted a number of broad issues relating to the development of youth work with young refugees which clearly merited further consideration.

As a result, the BMF further commissioned PVSD to undertake research into the youth work needs of young refugees for the following expressed purposes:

To determine

a) *the essential elements of an appropriate, relevant and effective youth work provision for refugee communities; and*

b) *to make recommendations to the BMF Management Committee on how it should proceed in influencing the provision and type of youth work and youth work training in the capital (from initial brief).*

Section One:

BACKGROUND

An Overview

Few topics attract so much attention in contemporary Britain as that of refugees and asylum seekers. It is impossible to read newspapers or listen to radio or watch TV without an awareness of the 'burdens' that refugees are seen to impose on British society. Much legislative effort has been devoted to issues of control, dispersal and detention and to policies to prevent 'bogus' refugees from living off the fat of the land.

A more careful examination of the media, however, presents a very different story. It has been widely reported that many refugees who are now settled in Britain were persecuted in their home countries. This suggests that many asylum seekers had legitimate reasons for coming to Britain. More subtly, 'success' stories about people who have contributed or are contributing to modern Britain in many ways often involve those who came to Britain as refugees many years ago. These stories often relate to refugees or the children of refugees who came to Britain in the 1930s (Jews) or in the 1960s/70s (Asians from East Africa). Often left out of these stories are the levels of hostility which British society directed at these refugees.[1]

One question rarely raised in the current debates about refugees and asylum seekers is: 'How can today's refugees become the successes of tomorrow?' A related question is: 'Are refugees and asylum seekers problems in themselves, or are they potential assets?'

These questions are central to a study of the youth work needs of young refugees because:

---

[1] An illustration of inconsistent attitudes is the two page spread in the London *Evening Standard*, 22 June 2000. Entitled "The capital's Asian Tiger millionaires", the article celebrated the success of six self-made Asian entrepreneurs. From the biographies of the six individuals, it was clear that at least two were from East Africa. This article was run at a time when the paper was regularly running stories of 'bogus' asylum seekers.

- Government, policy-makers and the media tend to be so obsessed with control/dispersal, etc., that they leave very little space for initiatives that promote inclusion and growth. This is most apparent during the first few years of refugee arrival. As it is accepted that early experiences can be decisive for later behaviour in many circumstances, there is no reason to believe this to be different for refugees.
- Often the declared agenda of control, etc., prohibits and discourages inclusion and growth.
- Policy-makers define refugees as a problem for whom and to whom things should be done. This means that policy fails to take account of the highly positive roles that refugees and their organisations can play.
- Refugees have very real problems but they also have strengths like everyone else.

Refugee organisations often carry much of the burden of their members' problems but they need support to develop the strengths inherent in their communities.

The current climate inhibits healthy discussion within refugee communities or between refugee communities and the 'host' community. For example, there are real issues on the place of small ethnic/cultural minorities in British society. Is the aim inclusion or integration and if so, what do these mean? Issues such as culture clash or generational conflict are also submerged in what is seen from the perspective of refugee organisations as a fight for survival. Beleaguered communities rarely have the luxury to examine sensitive but potentially divisive questions.

This study goes well beyond mundane issues such as recreational activities for young refugees. Youth work can have a decisive role in assisting young refugees in their adjustment to British society. It can also give a signal to more established refugees in Britain that this is a society that supports their endeavours to make a success of their lives in Britain.

The costs of the recommendations in this study pale into insignificance against the actual amounts currently spent on the many elements of control. Moreover, future costs can be saved by small expenditures now. For example, many police forces fear that bored unemployed young refugees are likely to be a major problem in the future. Therefore, any policy that reduces this threat can be seen to pay for itself. The benefit to society of integration and inclusion of young refugees at an early stage is likely to far outweigh initial expenditure. All the arguments, even the economic ones, favour a more civilised and constructive approach to the situation of young refugees.

Methodology

Background

Following work completed in 1998, the funders, the Barbara Melunsky Fund and partners and staff of Public and Voluntary Sector Development in Goldsmiths College, discussed how the work should be progressed. With the information from the earlier work, it was apparent that while some information on youth work and young refugees was available, there was no overview or systematic information on which any policy initiatives or long-term plans could be developed.

It was agreed that a survey of current work and of the main issues facing youth work with young refugees was required.

These discussions became critical in January/February 1999 because of two factors. One was the new Asylum and Immigration Bill. This contained proposals that were believed to fundamentally affect the position of new young asylum seekers. The second was the increasing numbers of refugees, especially young, often unaccompanied refugees, arriving from Eastern Europe, especially from Kosova and former Yugoslavia.

Time and resources constrained the methodology of this research. A research plan was agreed in early March 1999. Because of the urgency of the situation, it was agreed that the research should be completed as soon as practically possible, by September/October 1999. A draft report was issued in October 1999. Further discussions were held and the Barbara Melunsky Fund agreed to fund the preparation of this final report.

As the available resources were limited and the relevant Goldsmiths staff already had a very full programme of work, a freelance consultant was brought into the discussions in February 1999 to assist in the design and all other aspects of the research. A limited budget was agreed in March 1999, and the research was approved.

Main Objects of the Research

It was agreed that:

1. The research be limited to the Greater London area. As the majority of refugees in the UK live in London, it was agreed that concentrating on London was justified.
2. The research would take a broad brush approach. As very little detail was known, the priority was to map the outlines of the situation. The study was seen as necessary to highlight situations and policies with regard to youth work and young refugees. The study was not expected to produce definitive

quantitative results of, for example, numbers attending youth work provision or the number of agencies providing services. Instead, the study has been designed to give a qualitative picture of the situation of young refugees with regard to youth work.

Methods Employed

A postal questionnaire was circulated to all statutory providers in London, to major identified voluntary youth work providers, and to a large sample of refugee community organisations. In addition, using network approaches, other identified providers were included in the postal questionnaire. It was anticipated that nil returns or low response rates could be indicative of levels of activity.

The postal questionnaire was designed to obtain a general measure of youth work provision and to identify specific issues. The response rate for postal questionnaires is usually low but it is a method of covering a wide number of individuals or organisations quickly and cheaply. The results of these surveys should only be seen as general indicators and not as precise measures. This was anticipated from the outset and was not seen as problematical as it was already suspected that youth work activity for young refugees was very limited.[2] Additionally, the case study aspects of the research were seen as supplementing the broad detail expected from the questionnaires. Details of particular questionnaires and response rates are given in the appropriate sections.

Central to this research were the attitudes and needs of young refugees. While a random sample would have been optimal, this would have been very difficult for many reasons (see below). Instead, a series of group interviews with young refugees was used, with the interviews conducted by specially recruited refugee interviewers. While the results of this part of the research cannot be seen as definitive, they are indicative of some of the range of needs and issues as seen from the viewpoint of young refugees. A more definitive view would require much further research.

As we wanted to compare the views of young refugees with the views of refugee community organisations, the postal questionnaire was intended to provide an overview. In addition, a group interview was organised with 12 coordinators of refugee community organisations. The aim was to explore topics too complex for a simple questionnaire context. As a check, a further group of refugee youth workers was interviewed in a group situation. The refugee youth workers were seen as likely to be in a position midway between the young people and the coordinators.

---

[2] From previous work by the authors in both youth work and the refugee sectors.

As invitations were sent to coordinators, the group interviews consisted entirely of those who accepted an invitation to attend. It is not claimed that the views expressed by the coordinators or those expressed by the refugee youth workers are representative of all members of these groups in London. Every attempt was made to create wide ranging groups for these interview sessions, in order to represent a wide range of opinion. For reasons of time and economy, as well as the huge difficulty of creating sampling frames, the study opted for these methods in representing these viewpoints. Similar methodology and reasoning was used to hold a full-day event to explore the views of some mainstream (non-refugee) youth workers on their work with young refugees.

Finally, to supplement the research and to put more flesh on the bone, several individual interviews were carried out. These included four long in-depth interviews with senior workers in London youth work projects involved with young refugees. In two cases, the senior worker had been a recent asylum seeker. Workers from a major government funded agency with a brief for work with refugees were interviewed as well.

Throughout the research, the research team has used contact lists of youth work agencies, refugee community organisations and workers with whom they have had previous contact. While the research study has gone well beyond the confines of these earlier contacts, it would have been impossible to have gained the cooperation of such diverse groups in such a short period of time without these prior contacts.

Following the production of the draft report, informants were shown the section of the draft report to which they had contributed. This was as a check on the research method and to ensure that we had not misinterpreted the information gathered.

One of our original research aims remains to be done. We had hoped to survey the careers of refugees who have obtained youth and community qualifications in the past 15 years. While it was known that a number from different communities have obtained professional qualification, it is not known whether they have obtained posts in the youth and community services. Mainly for reasons of time and resources, no survey has yet been carried out.

Summary of Main Research Objectives

- To map out the main youth work provision for young refugees in Greater London.
- To assess which types of agencies (statutory or voluntary youth work, refugee community organisations, etc.) were the main providers.

- To gain some indication of what type of work with young refugees was being provided by different types of agencies, and to assess the range of provision.
- To obtain from young refugees some understanding of the role of existing youth provision in their lives.
- To gain from young refugees their own view of their overall youth work needs.
- To gain an understanding of issues affecting young refugees from their viewpoint.
- To examine the strengths and difficulties of all forms of youth work with young refugees.
- To describe the detail of what work with young refugees might involve.
- To examine the training needs involved in the further development and expansion of youth work with young refugees.
- To raise the profile of youth work with young refugees both with refugee communities and the mainstream providers of youth services.

The Main Sources of Information

For more detailed descriptions see below.

Questionnaires

Type of organisation	Number sent	Response	Response rate %
Local authorities	33	14	42
Voluntary YW providers	30	12	40
Refugee comm. orgs (RCOs)	78	24	31
Refugee umbrella orgs	23	4	17

Group Interviews

Type of group	No of groups	Total participants
Young refugees	9	59
Coordinators (RCOs)	1	11
Refugee youth workers	1	3
Mainstream youth workers	1	7

Additional Sources

- ⋆ Individual interviews with four senior youth workers and two workers from a refugee umbrella organisation.

Refugee Groups Included in Research:

Nationality of group	RCO questionnaire	RCO interview	Refugee youth workers' group interview	Young refugee group interview
Albanian/Kosovan				yes
Afghan	yes	yes		
Algerian				yes
Armenian		yes		
Congolese	yes			
East European	yes			
Eritrean	yes	yes	yes	
Ethiopian	yes	yes		
Iranian	yes		yes	yes
Kurdish incl. Turkish, Iranian, and Iraqi	yes			
Latin American incl. Colombia and Equador	yes	yes		
Somali	yes	yes	yes	yes
Tamil	yes	yes		
Ugandan	yes			yes
Vietnamese	yes			yes
Zairian	yes			

'Youth Work Needs of Young Refugees': Our Definitions

- *"[Young refugees] desperately need a welcoming atmosphere, love and security."* (refugee youth worker)
- *"Young refugees share the dynamics of all young people: they need to express themselves through music, for instance; they need role models; they need to*

experiment; they need assistance towards independence and they need opportunities to lead. They need a holistic approach." (refugee youth worker)

- *"Youth work is a luxury and an issue of settlement. Our work with refugees and asylum seekers is concerned with survival, with destitution."* (officer of large national organisation working for refugees and asylum seekers)
- *"Most refugees are excluded from the wider resources of the borough. They need access to resources and they are a resource too – they can contribute to the wider community. Integration is not about losing culture, it's about appreciation and mutuality."* (refugee youth worker)

In seeking to explore the 'youth work needs of young refugees' through this research, it is important to clarify our meanings in terms of 'young refugees', 'youth work' and 'youth work needs.'

Defining 'Young Refugees'

Young refugees and asylum seekers are not a homogenous group. Our definition of young refugees includes young people between the ages of 8 and 25 years, from over 20 countries and speaking many languages. It includes young people who have been in this country for a few months, a few years, or who have been born here as children of refugees. It includes those who arrived here as 'unaccompanied children' and those who came with their families. It includes young people living in ordinary homes with parents, with other members of their families, with friends from their own communities, or alone. It includes some living in hotels, hostels, 'looked after' in children's homes or foster homes. It includes those who are homeless. It includes those whose permanent or temporary residence in the UK has been approved and those whose application for asylum is currently being considered.

In researching and discussing the 'needs' of young refugees, the enormous diversity of need among this diverse group of people must be clarified. For the purposes of this research we are focusing on the 'youth work needs' of young refugees. What do we mean by this?

Definitions of Youth Work

The following Statement of Purpose for youth work was adopted in 1992 at a Ministerial Conference on youth work:

The purpose of youth work is to redress all forms of inequality and to ensure equality of opportunity for all young people to fulfil their potential as empowered individuals and members of groups and communities and to support young people during the transition to adulthood. Youth work offers young people opportunities which are:

- **Educative:** enabling young people to gain the skills, knowledge and attitudes needed to identify, advocate and pursue their rights and responsibilities as individuals and as members of groups and communities locally, nationally and internationally;

- **Designed to promote equality of opportunity:** through the challenging of oppressions such as racism and sexism and all those which spring from differences of culture, race, language, sexual identity, gender, disability, age, religion and class; and through the celebration of the diversity and strengths which arise from those differences;

- **Participative:** through a voluntary relationship with young people in which young people are partners in the learning process and decision-making cultures which affect their work and other young people's lives and their environment;

- **Empowering:** supporting young people to understand and act on the personal, social and political issues which affect their lives, the lives of others and the communities of which they are a part.

  (2nd Ministerial Conference for Youth Work in England and Wales, 1992)

The Thompson Report (DES 1982) offered four essential characteristics of youth work: "An experiential curriculum; participation in decision making; voluntaryism; and non-directive relationships between adults and young people." We believe these to be still relevant today. Taking each in turn:

1. *An experiential curriculum:* youth work is concerned with 'learning through doing'.

   It offers meaningful and challenging experiences for young people and support and challenge to reflect on these experiences, to learn through them and to test their learning out in further, often more challenging experiences. This is not the knowledge based learning of formal education, rather a process of developing knowledge of self, of and in the world, through meaningful, enjoyable and reflective activity. We call this Social Education.

2. *Participation in decision making:* an important part of this educative process is the way in which young people are encouraged and enabled to learn through

active involvement and participation in the actual activity of organising and implementing their programmes. In this way, youth work develops self-confidence and esteem and, most important, leadership skills.

3. ***Voluntaryism:*** young people are free to participate. They do so because they want to. Any form of compulsion can undermine and interfere with the learning activities and processes described above.

4. ***Non-directive relationships between adults and young people:*** young people are frequently at the interface of authoritarian adult relationships. As adults without statutory jurisdiction, youth workers negotiate their authority with young people. Youth workers have the young person's whole wellbeing at heart; are not seeking to control them but rather to assist them towards becoming self determining, responsible adults. Youth workers respect, value and trust young people and believe passionately in their potential. They have a depth of knowledge and understanding of the range of issues in young people's lives as well as concrete interests, skills, networks and resources to share with them.

Defining 'Youth Work'

The term 'youth work' has increasingly been used as a catch all for any work with young people which does not fall within the statutory jurisdiction of formal education, social services, housing and youth justice, and, in the case of young refugees, those agencies involved with the asylum seeking process. **We do not use the term in this way**.

It is our view that youth workers do not do the work of lawyers, teachers, social workers, housing providers or the police. Teachers, social workers, housing workers, and the police may sometimes do youth work, however.

For example, in the course of our research, we heard of a hotel in one London borough which currently provides temporary housing for a large number of young male Kosovan refugees. The local police were worried about the possible consequences of the levels of boredom experienced by these young men-in-waiting, living in cramped conditions without any source of income. So they organised a football tournament, pitching their own police team against teams made up from the hotel. In doing this, they were demonstrating a broader concern for the wellbeing of these young refugees.

This football tournament may have been a 'drop in the ocean' in addressing the vast range of these young men's needs. However, in challenging the young men to a game the police were challenging the young men to organise themselves. They were asked to work together cooperatively, to develop relationships with each other, to take healthy exercise, to develop and practice their skills, to prove what they can do, to mix socially with members of the 'host' community and to access resources in the local area. This football game is likely to have had a range of very positive outcomes for these lonely, isolated young men

In this example, it would have been highly constructive if the police had built on the football initiative, perhaps through access to youth workers or the local youth service.

The 'Youth Work Needs of Young Refugees'

In seeking to assess the 'youth work needs' of young refugees therefore, we have been researching:

- young refugees' diverse social, personal, political and emotional development needs – those needs which are unlikely to be met by the statutory services;
- the youth work possibilities and opportunities available for young refugees: wherever there are young people, in a hostel or a supplementary school, for example, there are opportunities to develop youth work;
- what is needed to enable youth work with young refugees to develop? What policies will encourage it? What is needed to develop the skills and attributes of adults to develop it and lead it? Where can the resources be found to support it? Effective youth work needs a supportive environment if it is to flourish.

Section Two:

CONSULTING YOUNG REFUGEES

This research study centres on the needs of young refugees. While it was clear from the outset that the views of young refugees must be gathered in order to identify these needs, several problems had to be faced. First, resources were very limited and the time period was short.

Second, young refugees are not a homogenous group. This meant that many standard methods of surveying would not be appropriate. Because of language problems and the complexity of issues to be explored, a standard questionnaire was considered but rejected as inappropriate. Individual interviews following a structured interview format were also considered. However, these were seen as inappropriate for reasons of expense and time, and also because they could arouse suspicion on the part of interviewees. It was realised that as many refugees are anxious about their UK asylum status and their very negative experience of officialdom in their countries of origin, they might be suspicious of any personal questions and might well refuse to answer many questions. It was therefore decided to use a method of group interviews.

Methodology

As our main concern was 'Developing Youth Work with Young Refugees', it was decided to focus on interviews with young refugees who were in touch with some form of youth work provision (widely defined). The main issues were to be discussed in group interviews. A team of interviewers, mainly of refugee origin, and all with some experience of youth work or working with young people, was recruited and trained for the task (see below). In addition, as a check on those present at interviews, a short and very simple questionnaire was developed for all taking part in the group interviews. This questionnaire specifically asked respondents **not** to give their names or any identifying information.

Recruitment of Interviewers

Several organisations working with refugee communities were approached with the aim of bringing together a team of refugee workers who wished to be trained to carry out the interviews with young refugees. The main criteria for selection to the team were:

- experience of working with young refugees;
- personal and professional interest in the subject of the research; and
- availability to undertake and complete the work.

Seven interviewers were engaged from the Albanian, Algerian, Eritrean, Ethiopian, Kurdish, Somali and African-Caribbean communities. Most of these were actively involved in youth work with young refugees and/or as community language teachers. The African-Caribbean interviewer works for one of the few full-time refugee youth work projects in London; some had worked with young people as teachers in their countries of origin; and four were actively engaged in working with young people in refugee community organisations as paid or voluntary workers.

Training for Interviewers

The first meeting of the interviewers was held to develop a cohesive team. Background and experience were shared as a way of getting to know each other. The sharing of common experiences informed subsequent discussions about the nature and form of the interviews. Draft questionnaires and interviewer checklists were then scrutinised by the interviewers and developed through discussion. Guidelines for interviewing were proposed, discussed at length and amended accordingly. Confidentiality was established as a guiding principle. The research team then contributed to identifying groups of young people for interviewing.

Further interviewer meetings were held whilst the research was being undertaken. This provided opportunities for additional support, training, and, most important, feedback. These meetings enabled the interviewers to familiarise themselves with the research tools, share their experiences, and plan how best to conduct the interviews. They also explored the effectiveness of different techniques for breaking the ice and facilitating frank and open discussions with new young people.

A third and final part of this process consisted of a meeting to reflect on the experience of the research. There was much positive feedback and learning. In general the interviewers reported a high level of excitement amongst the young people who, they felt, could have talked all night. Much of their learning was the discovery of needs amongst the young people that had not been recognised before.

The development of a team of refugee interviewers was a significant but not unexpected outcome of this research study. This team developed well, working intelligently together with a high level of commitment and reliability. As the team is keen to continue, a more formal training programme leading to accreditation could usefully be built into future projects of this kind.

Selection of Groups of Young Refugees

The aim was to interview between eight and ten groups of young refugees. Twelve of them were targeted and nine were finally interviewed. There were considerable difficulties in setting up some interviews to fit in with the programmes of organisations, the availability of interviewers and the enthusiasm or lack of it on the part of the young people. The different target groups were drawn from organisations with which PVSD was in touch and selected to include a spread of nationalities and types of situation. It was decided to include two groups working with one of the very few detached youth work projects in London with a specific refugee brief. It was known that these two groups would include a very high proportion of young people living in hostels.

As interviewing took place in summer 1999 at the height of the crisis in Kosova, it was decided to interview two groups from Kosova. One group consisted of regular users of an Albanian youth action centre, while the other lived in a refugee hostel and had been contacted by the detached youth project (see above paragraph). For clarity throughout this research, the first group will be described as "AYA (Kosovan)", the second as "Kosovan". *In actual fact, all members of both groups are ethnic Albanian, speak Albanian and come from the region of Kosova, in former Yugoslavia.*

All the groups except one were of a single nationality/origin. The mixed group was interviewed at a secondary school in northwest London.[3] This group, which included three Somalis, one Eritrean and one Pakistani, will be referred to in the research as the "School" group.

The organisations contacted were given details of the research and asked to arrange interviews with a group of six to eight young refugees. No specification was made as to who should be present and it was stressed that the interview was entirely voluntary. Generally, workers from the project involved did not attend the group interview. To relax the atmosphere, interviewers provided some refreshments and light snacks for participants.

---

[3] The group is run by a voluntary organisation specialising in work with children of refugees and is based in a mixed comprehensive school.

Group Interviews

A checklist was prepared for the group interview. After discussion and amendment by the research team, the schedule was piloted during the training of the refugee interviewers. As a result of this, the schedule was further amended for clarity and to avoid ambiguity. The refugee interviewers contributed to the design of the checklist and at the same time familiarised themselves with its content.

Interviewers were instructed to introduce themselves, making clear their own status as refugees and youth workers. They should describe the research and its purposes. After that they should emphasise that the research did not seek to obtain any confidential individual information concerning participants.

Interviewers were to work in pairs, if possible with one interviewer from the same ethnic group/nationality as the group being interviewed. One interviewer, from a different ethnic group/nationality from the group, was to act as discussion leader while the other interviewer was to act as the main note taker.

The interviewers were to allow the discussion to be free flowing, checking at different points whether the views expressed held for all participants. It was quite acceptable if different viewpoints were expressed and interviewers did not have to establish consensus.

Following the group interview, the interviewers were to write up their report of the interview and return it to the research team. In addition, a session was arranged at the end of the interviewing process for all the interviewers to attend and discuss the experience. This session (described in the section on recruitment and training) was very positive and a number of points were enlarged in discussion. Some of this feedback is incorporated in the results below.

Questionnaire

A short questionnaire was designed to obtain some background information on respondents in each group interview. The questionnaire was tested out on the refugee interviewers during their training and amended for greater clarity and relevance. Interviewers were asked to assist those young people whose command of English was not good or who had confusion or doubts about meanings or answers.

The questions were basically factual to discover how long the young people had been in the UK and London, where they lived, etc. It also asked about their UK educational experience and included a few questions on their leisure activities and use of youth work provision. Interviewers reported that the majority of young people completed the questionnaire in less than 15 minutes. All interviewees completed questionnaires, though in one group, due to a photocopying error, one page was missed out for half the respondents.

The Groups

The following groups were interviewed:

Group	Venue	Numbers/Sex	Age range	Median age
Albanian AYA (Kosovan)	youth action centre	6 males	14 – 17	16
Algerian	comm'ty centre	12 males	19 – 25	23
Armenian	centre	3 males, 3 females	14 – 19	16
Iranian	detached youth project, at hostel	5 females	18 – 23	19
Kosovan	detached youth project, at hostel	7 males	17 – 26	18
Somali	comm'ty centre	1 male, 5 females	12 – 15	13/14
School	school	2 males, 3 females	all 12	12
Ugandan	youth project	1 male, 4 females	18 – 24	22
Vietnamese	comm'ty centre	7 females	11 – 17	13

Source: Questionnaires

All members of the Iranian and Kosovan group lived in hostels and had no family in the UK. The AYA (Kosovan) group, all born in Kosova, were all living in the community usually with relations such as uncles/brothers, etc.; none was living with parents. All of the Vietnamese group lived with family; all but one with parents and all for whom we have information lived in either local authority or housing association property. All of the Somali group were living with family, one with an older sister and the rest with parents. Similarly, all the School group were living with their parents. All but one of the Armenian group were living with their parents. Three of the Ugandan group lived with their families, while the other two lived alone – one in local authority housing and the other in a hotel. By far the most mixed in terms of housing were the Algerians; one was homeless, three lived in hostels (all recent arrivals), while most of the others shared accommodation with friends. Only one of the Algerians lived with members of their own family. Many of those living in the community in all groups were living in temporary accommodation.[4]

The length of time that the different groups had been in the UK varied greatly. In summary form:

Group	under 1 year	1 to 5 years	6 to 10 years	more than 10 years	born here
Algerian	3	7	2		
AYA (Kosovan)	6				
Armenian	2		1		3
Iranian		1	4		
Kosovan	6	1			
Somali		2	3	1	
School		4		1	
Ugandan			3	2	
Vietnamese		2	1		4

Source: Questionnaires

Quite clearly the amount of time the different groups have been in the UK affects most of the matters examined in this study. The information is useful in that it might be possible to predict the general direction in which the different groups may develop. In this sense the Vietnamese represented a group which is most settled in the UK, while the Kosovans and Albanians are the most recent arrivals.

The Armenians really represented two groups: three individuals were born in the UK to families that came to Britain some time ago, often via another country, while three others arrived in the UK following the turmoil in the post Soviet era. Thus, the Armenians remind us that a number of national and ethnic communities are a mixture of long settled, often quite small communities with recent influxes of refugees. Two examples are the Somalis and the Ugandans. The Somalis include long

---

[4] Throughout this section, we have mainly analysed the responses according to the groups/nationalities of respondents. We could have equally analysed responses by other criteria. For example, there are huge differences between those at school and those not in school, those with families and those alone, between males and females, etc. We hope that this method of analysis does not obscure these differences.

settled communities in East London, Liverpool and Cardiff, as well as many recent refugees from war; or a community like the Ugandans with a post 1945 core of ex-servicemen, students and refugees from Idi Amin as well as more recent refugees from civil war and unrest.

The educational experience of the different groups also varied greatly. Questions related only to respondents' education in the UK, not in their countries of origin. None of the Algerian group had been to school in the UK (*Note: no information on education was collected from seven Algerians – see above re photocopying problem*). Three had attended college in the UK, two on English as a Second Language (ESOL) courses. Four of the Iranians were attending college – two on English courses (none had attended UK schools). Six of the seven Kosovans, all recent arrivals, were attending English courses at a college. The AYA (Kosovan) group, also recent arrivals, were all attending school, except one. The one exception, the oldest, was going to college for English classes and training in IT. Similarly, all the Somali and School groups were attending school. All of the Ugandans had attended UK schools for between four and eight years. All had also attended college, some for A-levels, one for BTEC, one for an NVQ, one for a nursing qualification. All of the Vietnamese had attended UK schools, most for their entire educational experience. The most recent arrival in the UK (four years) was the oldest and was attending college to study for four A-levels. The Armenians had all attended school, while two were now at college.

Early Impressions of the UK

Not surprisingly, first impressions varied. There was a lot of negative comment on the weather: "*it keeps changing*" (Algerians), or "*cold*" "*very cold*" (Somalis, Ugandans and Vietnamese). One Somali said that it "*was so cold, I thought I was on another planet*". Others commented on the pollution and said that the "*Underground is dirty*" (Algerians), noted traffic on the left (Somali) and were fascinated by London landmarks like Tower Bridge and the Houses of Parliament (Albanian). The School group commented on England being "*very clean*" and having "*no dust*".

Reception by Immigration officials: this was a significant memory for all of the groups except those so young that their parents handled the main dealings. Some groups such as the Algerians mainly felt that the Immigration officers could be understood and did their jobs competently even though the respondents all said that they were frightened the first time they faced the Immigration Service. On the other hand, the Iranian women had a very negative first impression of the Immigration Service feeling they were not believed, that the officials thought they were pretending not to understand English or to have no passports or money. Interestingly, all the young women agreed that after the initial negative impression during the period when they had to establish their position, the officials became more relaxed, friendly and helpful. The Armenians commented on the very long waits at the Home Office. It was said that initially officials *"were not nice"*, but their attitude improved as the Armenians' command of English improved.

The Kosovans, on the whole, felt that Immigration had been helpful. One described England as *"a place of justice and that everything was going to be okay"*. The AYA (Kosovan) group was also positive about the Immigration Service. They were questioned about status and whether they were from Kosova or Albania and asked detailed questions. One of the AYA group said he knew he had to ask for asylum at Dover, but did not know whom to ask. He asked two uniformed men who bought him a phone card so he could phone his brother who was already in England; afterwards he realised the two men were rubbish collectors. He still carries that phone card.

Other early impressions: *"The police are the best in the world"* (Algerian) and an AYA (Kosovan) said: *"I felt free when I saw policemen respecting people"*. Many commented on how international and multiracial London was; this came as a surprise to many. They all commented in a positive way on the variety of people in London from all over the world.

All groups found the British system of authority difficult to understand at first. For most, the best sources of advice on education, language, housing, benefits and generally dealing with officialdom were fellow refugees from their own communities. A number also commented on help they received from refugees from other communities.

Considerable difficulty was experienced in filling in forms and help was often necessary; refugee community organisations and fellow refugees were particularly helpful here. Despite some informal sources of advice, a number felt that they did not get appropriate advice on how to deal with public bodies. One of the Iranian women was very positive about her caseworker:

"She gave me an image of the society I had arrived into. I didn't like my position, but people were respectful and helpful."

Generally, the Iranian women were positive about the sources of advice such as caseworkers and solicitors on asylum matters, hostel workers and caseworkers on housing/education and social security.

The Armenian, School, Somali, Ugandan and Vietnamese groups generally reported much less about their first and subsequent early impressions. This was partly due to the longer passage of time and that in most cases their parents dealt with the main issues. Groups talked about the difficulties of finding accommodation but one of the Vietnamese group said: *"Our house is better"*. One Somali remembered that when living in a hostel, a caretaker tried to help them but her mother was frightened to talk to him.

Generally the main adjustment to a new society for these groups was at school. The groups gave the educational system good marks for their reception. There were also a number of comments on the friendliness of fellow pupils and teachers. The School group named individuals who were *"very friendly"* and said most of the children in the school were very friendly. Other comments on education, nearly all from those in college, were positive about the relaxed manner of teachers, contrasting it favourably with what they had previously known.

In commenting on their initial periods in the UK, all the groups stressed the importance of learning English and that people's attitudes to them improved as they became more fluent in English. Many talked about their own frustration (currently or in the past) at not being able to express themselves fluently in English. Most talked about the difficulties of understanding the system (immigration law, social security, housing, etc.). Two of the recently arrived AYA (Kosovans) were living with an uncle who had been in the UK for ten years; they said he had taken them everywhere at first to help them settle in and this had been a huge help. All stressed how important it was to be able to meet and be with others who spoke their language and with whom they could share their experiences. Most found early advice and comfort from members of their own communities, either informally or in a facility such as a community centre.

How Young Refugees Spend their Time

All the groups were asked to discuss: With whom do you spend your time? Where do you spend your time? What do you do? The answers obviously varied considerably according to age; for those at school the routines of school dominated. For those who had either lived in Britain a long time or were born in the UK, the patterns of life were not significantly different from those of other young people. For more recent arrivals, especially those still living in hostels, very different patterns emerged.

Both the Kosovans and Iranians, all of whom lived in hostels, spent long periods alone in the hostel. There were serious tensions between one of the groups and the hostel management from social services. The ban on refugees working was felt particularly hard, especially when hostel workers indicated that a refugee *"should be grateful to the hostel as it was his [the worker's] tax money that paid for him."* With little to do, lack of money and feelings of dependency, they wanted to train for 'real' jobs.

Thus most of the Kosovans and Iranians spent the bulk of their waking time in the hostel. For those attending college, this was next in importance. Apart from hostel and college, most of the rest of their time was spent visiting friends and fellow refugees, reading, studying, watching TV and very often being alone. A number commented that they mainly watched TV to improve their English. For both these groups their main social contacts were fellow refugees, usually from their own communities.

The AYA (Kosovan) group, also recent arrivals, consisted of younger people living in the community. They spent most of their time at school and home, but school was clearly more important to them than college was for their compatriots in the 'Kosovan' group. In addition, the youth group at the community centre was very important. Most attended two or three times a week and met friends either at the centre or arranged to meet them elsewhere.

It is interesting to note that the AYA group came to the centre from all parts of London; members came from Earls Court, Homerton, Lewisham, Wandsworth and Westminster. This group mentioned a number of activities including sports like swimming, football, also using the Internet and playing guitar. The community centre provided some of these opportunities and provided books in Albanian. This group mentioned being alone far less than the Kosovan or Iranian group, although they did mention being homesick and fearful for their families in a war situation. This group also mentioned British friends more, probably a function of attending school and living in the community.

The Algerian group, the oldest (in terms of age) of the groups interviewed, had a very different lifestyle. Most of this all male group did not have families with them. They play football at weekends (often informal kickabouts in a park), go to gyms, go clubbing, meet in coffee shops and meet other Algerians. Some have been in the UK some time and are allowed to work. Many, however, spend a lot of time thinking and worrying about their refugee status and become very depressed. It was reported that there are splits in the community as resident Algerians, i.e. those with residence who can legally work, have very little to do with the newcomers. While there seemed to be an active social life within the Algerian community, it was said that they hardly speak about politics to each other because they are afraid of the consequences. For these reasons some Algerians mix very little.

The Somalis were another school age group and had been resident longer. They mainly spent their time at school, with family or friends in their own community. They all regularly attended the Somali youth project two or three times a week but no other clubs. None mentioned going to any clubs, bars, coffee shops or sporting activities.

The School group had similar patterns, four of the five attending school clubs such as homework, textiles and football club (a female). Two regularly attended national (Eritrean and Somali) community centres. One young Pakistani boy regularly attended a badminton club and a cricket club. Four out of five of this group attended religious classes or went to the mosque.

All the Somalis attended Islamic religious classes every week. In contrast, only four of the 12 Algerians mentioned going to the mosque. None of the Albanian, Kosovan or Iranian groups mentioned religious classes or services, though all of the above came from predominantly Islamic communities. From the other communities, four out of five Ugandans attended church regularly, three of the seven Vietnamese attended religious classes/services and one Armenian reported church attendance at Christmas and Easter.

Most of the Ugandan group attended school or college and spent most of their time there or at home with family. This group also spent a lot of time with members of their community but specifically mentioned school friends who are not members of their community. As they said, *"We practise our culture to preserve our culture and make our parents happy. We also practise British culture when we are with our British friends. We have different hobbies individually; we like African and British music; we have special African dance"*. They all regularly attended the project where they were interviewed, between once and three times a week. They also went on outings – to the sea in summer, outings in London, etc. One mentioned attending a jazz club but outside of church and project attendance nothing else was recorded.

The Vietnamese were all attending school or college so this occupied much of their time. Four also attended school sports clubs e.g., football, snooker, table tennis and gymnastics. Attendance at the community centre varied between once and four times a week. They talked about going to friends' homes, helping their mothers, looking after younger cousins, talking on the phone and watching TV. One said her mother wants her to work but as she is not yet 16 she cannot. Others said their parents wanted them to have a good education and would not allow them to work.

Three of the Armenians were born in the UK and said they did not consider themselves refugees. Two were involved in typical activities for English teenagers, such as school rugby (male), and football and pool at a youth club (female). One born in the UK came to the centre once a week to teach English to newcomers. Those born in the UK had friends from a number of cultures and took typical excursions, for example, to Blackpool. All of them attended the community centre weekly. The other three were busy studying at school and college. One who had been in the UK just under a year expressed the wish to join a club for sports but so far had not found anything suitable. The newcomers all said they socialised mainly with members of their own community and school and college friends.

The Good and Bad in their Lives

All the groups were asked about the major issues in their lives – the good and the bad. Safety was seen as the key positive, though expressed in different ways: *"We are safe, we have food and shelter"* (Kosovans). *"Out of the dangerous situation in our country"* (Iranians). *"London is a safe city. The system is strong"* (Algerians). *"Sleeping without feeling frightened"* (AYA Kosovans). The other groups did not cite issues of safety so strongly, probably because some had been born in the UK or left their countries of origin when very young. Comments referring to freedom (Vietnamese and Somalis) probably refer as much to their personal lives as to the political climate.

Quality of services was another positive factor. Education and health services were both praised by the Ugandans. The Vietnamese said, *"They teach us in a fun way, not like our country"* and *"The teachers give us extra help when we need it"*. The Somalis also reported *"more fun at school"* and *"many different learning activities to work with"*. The Armenians also liked school, as did the AYA Kosovans. The School group said: *"Education is very good"*. The Algerians did not comment on education but said: *"the police are wonderful"* and *"transport is excellent"*. The Somalis also thought that transportation was good and cheap. Generally, the Vietnamese thought that service was good and that people were treated in a polite manner. The Ugandans stressed that there were more opportunities in the UK.

A particular positive for some groups was meeting and making new friends and the multi-cultural mix of London. The AYA Kosovans, Algerians, Iranians and Somalis all talked about this. A number of members of groups talked about particular friends (girlfriends), often of different nationalities[5]. Others mentioned factors like sports, music, the parks, etc. A number of groups singled out attendance at the venue where they were meeting as one of the good things in their life. The opportunities that each of these venues (community centres, youth projects) afforded these young people were seen as valuable though to some the benefits were limited by their relative infrequency. For example, the Armenian group only met once a week.

For many of the groups the key 'bad' thing in their lives was missing their families and worrying about people left in their countries of origin (AYA Kosovans, Algerians,

---

[5] Interestingly, none of our female respondents talked about boyfriends.

Iranians and Kosovans). Among those who have been here longer, or where respondents were younger, comments concentrated on the mechanics of everyday life.

For example, the Somali group identified school-related issues as negative factors in their life. School uniforms (short skirts) were seen as bad for Muslim girls, along with racist remarks from some teachers, and no room for prayers (complaints that teachers did not take the request seriously). Another issue was school lunches: as refugees they are only entitled to £1.20 per day which often does not permit much choice in purchasing food and drink. Naturally this causes these young people to see themselves as different.[6]

Racism was a serious issue for a number of other groups as well. For example, the Ugandans said they were frightened when they were outside on their own and that racism can occur anywhere. The Vietnamese said: *"Racism is out of order"*, and some of the AYA Kosovans felt that teachers separate them and make racist comments. In a similar vein the Armenians felt that bullying in school was a problem as are gangs, name calling, racism and swearing. The School group said: *"Most British people are kind but some people are racist"* and that they *"are frightened when they go out at night"*.

The Kosovan group was the least satisfied by any measure. They complained about the hostel where they were living, especially the food and the hygiene. They also felt that they did not get enough help to train for a constructive career and that nobody listened to them as *"they had no say as refugees in this country"*. The Iranians expressed the need for Stage 2 housing so that they could move on from the hostel.

Another frequent comment was: *"No job, no money, can't go out, not active socially"* (Iranian). This comment was echoed in various ways by the AYA Kosovans, Algerians and Kosovans. Not working had repercussions, especially for the newly arrived who had to exist on £28 per week. This left many at a loose end. Two groups commented on the high cost of life in London.

The Quality of Life

All participants were asked to consider the overall quality of their lives. They were given prompts as to whether it was 'interesting', 'boring', 'lonely' and a scale of 'good', 'not bad/not good', 'bad'. The good to bad scale was in terms of 'considering being in a strange land'. Any other words could be used and multiple answers were acceptable.

---

[6] Many of the points raised in this section, especially those coming from younger refugees, are echoed in a survey of refugee youth in the London Borough of Greenwich in 1999. See YAPP (1999).

Responses varied between groups and within groups. For example, the Kosovan group was generally very negative. Five used the word 'boring' and also words and phrases like 'terrible', 'bad', 'rubbish', 'treated inhumanely', 'not what I thought'. But two were positive with 'OK' and 'good, considering being in a strange place'. The responses from the Iranian women, also living in a hostel, were also split with assessments of the overall quality of their life including 'horrible', 'lonely', 'boring' and 'interesting, not bad, not good'.

The AYA (Kosovan) group responses included 'boring' (2), 'not too bad', 'lonely', 'interesting' (2), and a thoughtful 'It depends on the day'. The Vietnamese response was more collective from the discussion and mentioned the seasons: *"In summer, we go out and have fun. In winter it is boring and we spend most of our time in school or at home"*.

The Somali response was mixed. Three said *"it is good because we live in an area where we can get support from our community"* (this group attended a local community centre with a fairly high population of Somalis). Some described their lives as interesting as they learnt new things and made new friends. Some said it was very bad and confusing when you do not understand and can't communicate with people. Also it was embarrassing not to know the language. Two said life was boring as they miss the rest of their family back home.

The School group gave a generally positive response and described life as 'interesting'. They mentioned success at school, fun, watching TV, etc. Two mentioned their mothers' loneliness and one said: *"Life is very good, my Mum tells me"*.

Most Algerians regard themselves as only temporarily in the UK. Some feel bored and find London hard to live in. They do not understand the system and find the quality of their life difficult. Some want to return home to families. One Armenian also got bored sitting at home. Others wanted to come to their centre more than once a week. Some commented that their families did not allow them to have boyfriends/girlfriends. In this context, a UK born Armenian said: *"The only one culture that Armenians carry through the generations is sexism, even though the environment they live in [London] has grown out of such ideas."* The Ugandans' response was that the quality of their life is not bad but not the best: *"It is up and down."* They also explicitly mentioned a recurring issue in the responses of other groups: *"Sometimes we are very depressed because it is very difficult for us to find jobs."* This group also commented that teachers did not think they were as good as white students and that this upset them.

Young Refugees and Youth and Community Provision

In both the questionnaires and the discussion, the young people were asked about their use of youth provision. In the questionnaire they were asked how often per week they attended the youth provision/centre where the interviews took place. The results were as follows:

Numbers attending (times per week)

	Fewer than 1	*1*	*2*	*3 or more*
Albanian	–	2	2	2
Algerian	–	2	5	3
Armenian	–	6	–	–
School	1	2	2	
Somali	–	1	1	4
Ugandan	1	–	1	3
Vietnamese	1	2	–	3

Note: Persons not responding have been excluded.

Source: Questionnaires

Neither the Iranian nor Kosovan groups answered the question about attendance at youth provision/centres. The detached youth project dealing with refugee hostel dwellers worked with them either in their place of residence or took them out into the community.

Non-users

Two of the young Kosovan men knew of youth clubs but none attended. Three felt that they were too old and that they could play pool at the back of the coffee bar in the hostel. Three felt that they would like to go to a club where they could engage in activities such as football and also get taken around London.

None of the Iranian women attended any youth club and did not feel that they could get any help not obtainable elsewhere. This was expressed after a discussion in which they had talked about the need for mixing, learning the language and their need for (what could be defined as) informal education such as information on health care and issues like protected sex. One Iranian woman had registered at a local sports centre but the costs were too great for her to use the facilities. In discussion, it was found that these young women had a very limited view of the potential facilities that could be provided by a local youth and community project.

Users – Why Do They Attend?

While the responses varied both within groups and between groups, some thoughts were expressed by all groups, even if the form differed. The need to meet other members of their communities was seen as central; this was expressed in purely social terms or in terms of language, culture or religion. Every group saw attendance as a way of meeting their own very special needs. But, for nearly every group, attendance satisfied a number of other needs. It might be the opportunity to make friends, to go on outings and explore London and the UK, to participate in sporting activities or music, or to learn skills or something else. Attendance was also seen as a key element of support by these young people, providing a fixed point to meet others regularly.

Some of the provision is very specific. The Somalis said they came to the centre for religious studies and to learn their mother tongue. But they also came to socialise and share experiences with friends. They acknowledged that the centre's main purpose was learning, but they would like to have facilities for other activities like swimming, dance, traditional handicrafts, etc. The Somali girls said that the boys have football, but they have nothing to do.

The learning aspect of centres was very apparent. Responses from the AYA group included: *"To learn journalism by helping publish our newsletter"* and *"My favourite activity is to get foreign news from the Internet and to learn how to use the Internet."* Learning about one's own culture is an important element of these centres. The Ugandans stressed their cultural identity and dancing and singing while the Vietnamese saw different cultural activities as an important part of the programme. The Armenian group said that it was the only place they could come to speak their language, possibly reflecting that some of those attending are well established second generation. The facilities at the Algerian community centre were very limited but respondents acknowledged the importance of English classes.

Fun is also on the agenda. The Vietnamese came for fun and to gossip with friends. The Armenians talked about fun and entertainment. Outings to the cinema, to swimming baths, to venues in London and the seaside were on the agenda for at least five of the groups we interviewed. In nearly all cases, there was demand for more resources to step up this part of the programme.

It is clear that the centres meet a multiplicity of needs, even if they only satisfy them in part. Comments on lack of space, facilities, staffing and resources were common. The reasons why young people's needs were not being met seemed to have more to do with insufficient resources than cultural restraints within the refugee communities.

Users – What Help Do Young People Get?

After asking the groups 'Why do you come to the club?' we attempted to focus answers by specifically asking, 'In what ways does coming to the [club] help you in your life in Britain?' Not surprisingly, there was considerable overlap in the answers. This line of questioning amplified earlier answers and provided a focus for the role of centres. For example, the Somalis said that coming to the club and meeting new friends allowed them to learn from fellow refugees what is going on in their borough. Teachers (religious) at the club often informed them what was going on in the world and of the suffering back home. They also said that the club gave them the opportunity to discuss TV programmes related to refugees. Similarly, the Vietnamese group explained that the centre runs mother tongue classes for them and English classes for their parents. They thought the mother tongue classes were important as it was difficult to keep up both your own language and English.

Many of the groups gave much more explicit input about the advice role of centres. The Ugandans saw the youth centre as supplying advice on education and other issues affecting young people. The Algerians saw their centre as a source of advice and information on issues such as immigration, asylum appeals, housing benefit, etc. The AYA (Kosovans) found their centre gave them help in finding schools and colleges, advice on benefits, social services and travelcards.

Groups raised issues relevant to their own centres. The AYA (Kosovans) gave the most detailed replies. They said they learnt to paint and do artwork and drama. They also said that they learnt to work together on projects like producing a newsletter and discussed HIV, drugs and all the problems of modern society. As one of them said: *"Because my family is not in the UK, I feel like this centre is my home. I am supported and welcome here. Coming here is like I am at home."*

Users – What Do They Want?

Several issues have already been raised in the sections above. It was common for the young people to comment on the lack of resources of their centre, of limited opening hours or of limitations of space and facilities.

A number of groups were quite explicit in their desire to have access to some very normal activities – no different from those that are available to young people normally resident in the UK. More opportunity for trips around London and to the rest of the country was a particular desire. Many of these young refugees have very limited financial resources and these opportunities would be particularly valued and educative. A number of groups talked about the possibility of having greater opportunity to participate in sports, particularly swimming and football, but basketball, snooker and pool were all mentioned. Individuals raised questions around greater access to the arts, to music and drama. At the Armenian centre, a volunteer paid out of her own pocket to take children to the theatre.

Many, not surprisingly, noting the emphasis that so many of these centres put on education, wanted more education. Most basic was the need for English classes. For example, the Algerians could afford only one teacher and the demand was greater than the supply. Others, notably in the Armenian group, wanted to extend the range of mother tongue and cultural learning. Others wanted to learn how to use computers and the Internet; a number of groups did not have the equipment.

While the range of activities on offer is limited, the range of items on the young people's wish lists is also fairly limited. This is not surprising when one realises that the experience of these young people is nowhere near as wide as that within an average community in the UK. Most well established youth centres and clubs can offer a range of activities well beyond the experience of most of the young people we interviewed. Outdoor pursuits, adventure expeditions and many crafts are not within the experience of young refugees. The variety of arts and drama capable of being pursued is vast and it will be a tragedy if young refugees, because of lack of knowledge, cannot develop their skills. There has been an upsurge of minority sports in Britain in the last decade. If football is all that is offered to these young people, that would be a pity.

Consulting Young Refugees: Findings

Refugees generally find their greatest source of support, advice and help from fellow refugees, especially among those who arrived earliest and are more established. This is also true of young refugees, including the children of refugees.

More specifically, our research with young refugees found that:

1. Centres, usually provided by refugee organisations, are seen as a major source of support, general advice and help.
2. Young refugees benefit from venues where they can meet others from a similar background. These venues often provide a number of social functions.
3. Young refugees without families in the UK are particularly vulnerable and have special needs for places of safety where they can mix with others from a similar background, speak their own language and discuss common problems.

4. There is a particular problem for young refugees living in hostels. At a time of maximum vulnerability, they have little access to sources of advice and support. Major problems of very little money, loneliness and boredom need to be addressed.

5. Young refugees have a range of needs and interests specific to the fact that they (and their families) are recent arrivals in the UK. These needs differ from refugee group to refugee group and between different individuals in the same group. These may include:

- English language classes and English conversation;
- Knowledge, advice and guidance concerning different aspects of UK society such as the educational system, health services, law and order, etc. Young refugees with no family support will need access to a much wider range of advice and guidance services;
- Religious instruction;
- Classes/activity in aspects of the cultural background of the refugee group including music and dance, traditional crafts, history, general news, etc.;
- Mother tongue classes.

6. Young refugees have a range of needs and interests very similar to those of many other young people. Among those reported during the research were:

- The need to relax and have fun with friends, to meet new people, etc.;
- The wish to enjoy and/or try out different sports and activities, including football, swimming, basketball, table tennis, gymnastics, snooker, pool, etc.;
- The opportunity to enjoy and discover a wide range of artistic and cultural activities;
- The chance to go out from a centre to take trips to different places in London and the rest of the country;
- The wish to learn a number of different skills including the playing of musical instruments, learning to use computers and the Internet and much else;
- All of the centres visited were poorly resourced. Young people complained of problems of space and general funding.

7. While there are some general issues affecting young refugees, methods of dealing with actual problems will vary greatly according to the circumstances.

No single policy can expect to encompass the needs of the newly arrived and of longer term residents, of those living with their families and of those unaccompanied, of those from a highly religious background and of those from a secular background. All policies must be flexible enough to adapt to the very different circumstances of each situation.

8. The team of refugee interviewers exceeded expectations in its level of involvement, its pace of development and, most important, its effectiveness. This positive outcome should be regarded as a significant aspect of this research study.

Section Three:

CONSULTING REFUGEE COMMUNITY ORGANISATIONS (RCOs)

In March 1999, 78 postal questionnaires were sent to a broad selection of refugee community organisations (RCOs). The questions concerned the nature of their work with young people and their resource and staffing needs. We hoped to develop a broad picture of the actual kinds of work taking place in RCOs, the extent to which young refugees' broader social and personal development needs were being addressed, and the levels of support currently offered to RCOs in terms of finance, staffing and other resources.

Five refugee youth workers and 11 coordinators of RCOs have been interviewed in groups and individually. These interviews had three aspects:

- first, these workers' perceptions of the youth work needs of young refugees within their own communities;
- second, the kinds of interventions which they would need to address these issues;
- third, their experiences of developing youth work with young refugees and the kinds of support and resources that they feel are needed.

Youth Work in Refugee Community Organisations: The Postal Questionnaire

Respondents

The 78 RCOs were asked to provide details of programmes and activities offered for young people aged between 8 and 25 years as well as information about how these activities were staffed and resourced. Space was left for additional comments on youth work provision.

As response was slow, a reminder was sent in late April. By the end of May responses were received from 24 refugee community organisations, a return of 31 per cent. In addition, two organisations which exist to support and enhance the work of RCOs responded. These are included in this section of the report.

A good cross section of the refugee communities in London is represented by the range of respondent organisations (number of multiple returns in brackets): Turkish, Iraqi and Iranian Kurds (4), Somali (3), Afghani (2), Tamil (2), Vietnamese (2), Zairian, Congolese, Ugandan, Kenyan, Zambian, Eritrean, Ethiopian, Latin American including Colombia and Ecuador, Iranian, Armenian, and East European, and one 'umbrella' organisation which serves 'all communities' with Somalis as its largest membership group. It is helpful that longer established communities (for example, the Vietnamese and Armenian) are considered alongside more recent arrivals.

Locality

Fourteen of the 24 organisations stated that they serve the whole of Greater London and of these, three stated that they work nationally. Of the remainder: three serve community members in North London, three in West London, one in East London and three in South London. Only one organisation stated that its work was confined to one London borough (Greenwich). The fact that RCOs' work extends beyond borough boundaries is significant when considering the nature of youth work:

- regular contact with young people living across the whole of London must be difficult for an organisation to maintain;
- young people, who frequently have few financial resources, may find it difficult to travel to find provision within their communities;
- London borough youth services, seemingly the most obvious source of support for youth work with young refugees, may be reluctant to support a pan London service or one which overtly extends its work to young people in other boroughs.

Activities for Young People

RCOs were asked to provide details of programmes aimed solely at young people. They were asked to distinguish between 'youth work' activities (leisure, sport, art, music etc.) and other forms of provision (e.g. advice, counselling, mother tongue classes, supplementary schooling etc.). A very varied and positive picture emerged.

Overall 20 organisations offer some kind of provision for young people, almost 77 per cent of respondents.

Of the 20, 14 organisations stated that they offer informal (i.e. youth work) activities exclusively for young people, almost 54 per cent of respondents. A very broad range of informal activity is offered (numbers of responses in brackets):

- sexual health workshops [2]; HIV/AIDS prevention [2], condom distribution [1]
- folk dancing [3], and dance [1]
- sport (not specified) [4], football [6], tak wan do [1]
- music [3], music band [1]
- art & painting [2]
- drama [1]
- holiday playschemes [3]
- summer holidays [2]
- advocacy [1]
- luncheon club [1], youth provision [3], out of school activity [1]

One organisation (serving one of the more established communities in London) provided its terms of reference for youth provision which address the rights of representation of young people in the organisation and on its youth committee.

The most varied youth work programmes were to be found in the Somali, Eritrean, Armenian and Kurdish organisations – some of the longer established groups.

Twelve of the above, alongside the remaining six (18 in total) offer a broad range of activities which fall into three main categories (numbers of responses in brackets):

- *formal education:* supplementary schooling and language support [10], mother tongue classes [7], homework clubs [2], after school classes [1];
- *advice, information and counselling:* resettlement [1], housing [4], schooling [2], interpretation & translation [3], HIV prevention [2], education, employment and training [3], counselling [2], casework [7], 'complex family problems' [1];
- *cultural events:* celebrations [3], cultural family events [4], "hall service for children on Christmas Day" [1].

Of the remaining six respondents, two stated that they provide for young people in the course of their generic advice work, and four gave a 'nil' response to all questions about activities for young people.

Age, Gender, Numbers and Hours of Provision

Organisations were asked to provide information concerning the nature and extent to which young people use the activities and services on offer.

Whilst most organisations provide activity for mixed gender groups, there is a tendency towards greater usage by boys and young men, especially in sport (roughly averaging seven boys to three girls). Some single sex work is offered, especially in the Somali community organisations. All three of these respondents stated that they offer single sex provision.

As organisations tended not to give detailed information about the age ranges of the young people with whom they work, it was difficult to gauge the level of activity offered for older children and young people. Where responses were forthcoming, informal provision is often targeted across the full range of 8 to 25 years; supplementary education tends to be targeted at 8 to 16-year-olds, and advice and information services tend to be used by over 16s.

On average, organisations offer between three and seven hours per week for exclusive work with young people. Seven organisations cited a much higher level of provision between 18 and 84 hours per week. All of these have paid staff dedicated to working with young people. Added together, the 20 organisations state that they are working with 3,163 young people, 1,415 of whom are engaged in informal youth work activities. In activities such as sport, drama, music, and 'youth provision', the average attendance for specific activities is between 20 and 30 young people. In formal education activities the numbers are higher: mother tongue classes average 40 to 50 and supplementary education activities saw numbers in the 100s. Advice and information services are accessed by even greater numbers; one organisation quoted 500. For cultural events the numbers quoted range from 30 to 500.

While we acknowledge that the questionnaire may have elicited higher levels of response from organisations that are currently working with young people, we believe that the high response rates show not only demand but confirm the importance of the role of RCOs in providing for young people. The responses also demonstrate what can be done with relatively few resources and are a testament to the RCOs' commitment to young people (see section below on staffing).

Staffing

Organisations were asked for information about how they staffed their youth activities. We wanted to know the extent to which RCOs were able to employ paid staff, the extent of their use of volunteers, and the degree and level of experience and qualifications held by paid or volunteer staff.

Nine of the 26 organisations stated that they have paid staff with dedicated responsibility for working with young people. Of these five are full-time appointments. The level of volunteering is high. Fifteen of the 20 organisations working with young people use volunteers; eight of the nine organisations with paid staff also use volunteers; five organisations stated that all of their work with young people is conducted by volunteers, many of whom are parents of the young people. In the remaining seven organisations, work with young people was undertaken by 'generic' staff.

Job titles for paid workers include:

- Youth Outreach Worker [1]
- Employment and Training Officer [1]
- Youth Housing Officer [1]
- Family Support Worker [1]
- School Liaison Worker [1]
- Youth Manager [1]
- After School Worker [1]
- Youth Worker [2]

These job titles probably reflect the priorities of the particular organisation in terms of its focus for work with young people.

Volunteers are cited as being involved in mother tongue and supplementary education [6]; sport, music and art [3]; information and advice [2]; condom distribution [1]; HIV project [1]; health [1]; and for generic work [2].

It appears (though it is not always clear in the responses) that most supplementary and mother tongue teaching is undertaken primarily by volunteers. Two organisations provided job titles for volunteers; both were 'Youth Project Coordinator'. One organisation had a team of volunteers working with a Community and Youth Work student on placement (from Goldsmiths College). Only seven of the respondents cited the actual numbers of volunteers used; these seven organisations have a total of 48 volunteers working with young people. We believe this to be significantly high, another indicator of commitment to young people, and we feel that it would be interesting to compare the level of volunteering in RCOs with that in other mainstream youth projects.

Training and Qualifications

We asked the organisations to tell us about the qualifications of their staff. As many did not respond to this question, we assume that their staff do not hold specific qualifications for work with young people (though we are aware that many refugees actually hold a broad range of professional qualifications).

We found no instances of RCOs employing youth workers with a full professional qualification in youth work. Of the nine organisations with paid staff, two have qualified youth workers in post. Both of these hold a 'local qualification' i.e. a part-time youth work qualification. Other qualifications held by youth work staff included: teaching [3], football coach [1] and doctor [1].

Given the high level of activity with young people and the numbers of staff both paid and voluntary who are engaged in this activity, it would seem that youth work training is a necessity. Youth services have traditionally always depended on a high level of volunteering in youth work (see earlier section on 'definitions'), and the origin of its 'local qualification' lies in a historical commitment to training and developing local people for this work.

Additional Comments from RCOs

As will be seen from the next section of this report (Mainstream Youth Services), refugee community organisations are evidently the primary providers of youth work with young refugees in London. Some commented on this:

> "Mainstream youth provisions are not accessed by many refugees because they are not culturally appropriate for their needs. Refugee community organisations endeavour to fill this gap but they are usually penalised by lack of resources. This area needs serious development within refugee community organisations."
>
> "We have had to develop this ourselves. There is no specialist youth service [for our young people] in London."
>
> "There are very few services for young refugees and this reflects the inadequate support for refugees as a whole. However, young refugees need services that are targeted to help them adapt and successfully integrate into the community. These services must also be aware and sensitive to the difficult circumstances that refugees live in, e.g. lack of family support, lack of networks and friends, break in education. Provision therefore must be flexible and practical and meet needs of adapting and pursuing opportunities."

Many organisations recognised that more needs to be done:

"We do not have youth services in our organisation but we would like to develop it."
"I would like to see policy giving special attention to refugee youth as they usually have special needs."
"Special support should be provided further to enable them to cope with the challenges of living in the UK."

and that it is not just the young people who need attention:

"Parents also should be supported to share ideas around best dealing with their youth, living in an alien environment facing a lack of social support structures."

Some respondents also recognised the need for a holistic approach to developing work with young refugees:

"Young refugee people are more likely to be subjected to exclusion and bullying in schools and other problems related to education and careers. An education advisor, familiar with the Education Act and code of practice would be useful."
"Services such as housing, counselling, education and immigration are the main issues facing young refugees. There is little provision for these areas and there is little understanding of these issues from funders and statutory bodies."

Raising the Issues: Interviews with Coordinators of Refugee Community Organisations

Eleven coordinators of RCOs were interviewed. They represented organisations working with Eritrean, Ethiopian, Somali, Afghan, Armenian, Kurdish, Tamil and Latin American communities. The method of interview was open discussion. It focused on exploring the coordinators' perceptions in three key areas:

- the needs of young refugees in the community context;
- the nature of the work taking place with young refugees in RCOs and issues arising; and
- what support RCOs need to develop the work.

Discussions were led by an experienced youth work professional with notes taken by a colleague.

The Needs of Young Refugees in the Community Context

All of those interviewed agreed that it is not always possible to generalise about the needs of young refugees as these may vary from one community to another according to cultural diversity and the degree to which the community is established in the UK. Nevertheless, the following points gained a high level of consensus:

Young refugees have a range of specific personal support needs due mainly to the following factors:

- many who do not speak English find integration at school difficult;
- many young refugees have had disrupted education due to the situation at home;
- many have witnessed and/or experienced horrors and brutality;
- many are subjected to bullying in school and other environments;
- many experience racist behaviour;
- many are not entitled to benefits, thus placing extra pressure on families and support agencies.

The system here is often unable or unwilling to recognise these factors and therefore continues to fail young refugees. When young refugees fail to obtain the support they need to address these issues, they frequently react in a negative way. As a consequence they can be excluded from school or find themselves unsympathetically dealt with by public services and law enforcement agencies.

It was generally felt that the experiences of refugee families, and the process of integration into the UK, often puts these families under extreme pressure. This can affect their ability to deal with their young people. Whilst recognising that many of these factors are present in Britain as a whole (the generations clash, family breakdown, etc.), it was nevertheless felt that the specific circumstances of refugee families can make matters worse. The following factors were felt to be relevant to many refugee young people:

- Many families live in extreme poverty. This places extreme pressure on young people. (The changes in the 1999 Immigration and Asylum Act seem likely to make matters worse.)
- Young people growing up in families that have been traumatised by war often experience severe emotional deprivation. It was the opinion of many coordinators that child abuse cases are on the rise. Emphasis is placed by

RCOs on dealing with the immediate effects for parents rather than the knock-on effects for young people.

- Many young people occupy adult roles in the family without adult power. A number of participants described the potentially damaging effect for young people as they increasingly act as the family interpreters, e.g. during visits to the GP or parents' evenings at school. While it is very helpful to be able to call on the child or young person to interpret, this situation can result in young people devaluing their parents' skills in coming to terms with life in the UK and can vastly increase family tensions.

- Everyone interviewed saw the concept of "torn (or 'divided') cultural identity" as a major issue. Young people are torn between the home culture and the culture prevailing in British society. Young people spend all day in a British school environment and as they settle they may also form their primary social relationships outside of the community. This can cause additional tensions between young people and their parents who may feel that community identity is being threatened, and that their sons/daughters are exposed to negative impacts of 'British' culture.

- Many young people can internalise the prevailing racist attitudes in the wider environment and devalue the worth of their home culture. This can result in further tensions. Young people need both to be involved and to take pride in their own communities and home culture. They also need to feel free to socialise outside. One participant referred to this as the double alienation experienced by young people:

"Alienation within the family/community as they struggle to come to terms with their identity, plus an external alienation within society at large which does not accept them/or they do not fit in."

- It was felt that young people often lack positive role models within their communities and that this can exacerbate the problem of negative self-image.

The Nature of Work With Young Refugees in RCOs and Issues Arising

Most of the RCO coordinators interviewed saw their own organisation as best placed to understand and address the issues and support needs of young people in their communities.

About half of the coordinators' organisations had specific provision for young people. Some was recreational in nature whilst other activities focused on cultural events. One organisation offers a youth club and employs a youth worker. In most of the RCOs, services to young people were offered in the context of generic advice, education or employment services.

All interviewees, however, stressed the difficulties and tensions in approaching this work. The main tension exists in the relationships between adults and young people as discussed above. Adults themselves often experience the tensions of torn cultural identity through their dealings with their young people. As one respondent said:

> *"The inclination to enforce traditional values, to control young people, whilst at the same time trying to work to develop them."*

This urge in adults to control young people is often dominant:

> *"In our supplementary school the standard punishment is to ban the speaking of English,"*

and,

> *"The organiser of our youth club told the parents that their children were found smoking in the changing rooms – there was a backlash."*

Thus, some coordinators questioned whether young people were engaging in the life of the RCO of their own volition:

> *"Do our young people come for themselves or because their families bring them?"*[7]

This issue of 'cross cultural shock' (see page 45) is at the forefront of their concerns:

> *"Young people are challenging the community as they adopt local cultures here. The community has to take the challenge, to change, or the young people will leave,"*

and,

> *"What happens when our young people reject the community's advice?"*

---

[7] Unfortunately, we failed to ask this question when consulting young refugees (see Section 2).

Most of those interviewed expressed the concern of their communities when young people become involved in illicit activities:

"We need to offer things for young people who are involved in drugs etc."

However, they felt that the stigma attached to the use of alcohol, drugs and gambling meant that the problems were ignored or denied in some communities. (Only two RCOs responding to the questionnaire offer any form of drug or sex education). The negative effects of pressures on young people to conform are often not recognised by adults in the community:

"Who asks young people what they are feeling? Who looks out for them and listens to them?"

What is Needed to Support RCOs in Developing the Work?

Both the concern and the will to develop and expand the work are clearly present:

"We have to work for young people's participation by driving it and taking responsibility for it."

However, all of the organisations interviewed felt severely under-resourced in this area in terms of staffing and finance.

All coordinators were aware of the existence of their local youth services but varied in the degree of perception of the level of support offered. The minority was fairly or very satisfied with the level of support received whilst for most it was low or non-existent. The perception was that youth services were reluctant to target young refugees as a specific activity area, or simply did not have the resources.

All felt that concrete resources, in terms of finance, staffing and training, are essential for RCOs to develop their responses to young people. They expressed an urgent need for trained staff who could develop positive new approaches to working with the young.

It was further felt that statutory agencies need to improve access to their own services by better understanding the issues facing young refugees and developing the capacity to respond to language and cultural needs. One suggestion was exchanges between teachers in schools and those in supplementary schools.

Whilst the need for youth work with young people in refugee communities was strongly expressed, the coordinators identified a parallel need to develop approaches to working proactively with parents. Parents are often unaware or unsupported in their struggle to understand the need for sex education, to recognise the signs of drug abuse, and to learn about the implications of the Children Act and the UN Convention on the Rights of the Child.

"Parents need opportunities to discuss the issues: to talk about communication; explore what happens when young people leave home; think about sex education; learn about drugs ..."

Two further strategies were proposed:
- a back up referral service for specific support needs (e.g. access to counselling for young refugees); and
- the development of youth counselling services in schools.

Group Interview: Refugee Youth Workers

Twelve workers were invited to a group interview through the Refugee Youth Work Forum[8]. Three actually attended: an Iranian, an Eritrean and a Somali. They were asked to discuss their perceptions of the main issues in young refugees' lives and the kinds of support and activities needed.

Issues for Young Refugees

In common with the RCO coordinators, the group talked at some length of young refugees' experiences in school and focused on the following:

- Being put in a classroom with a same age peer group but not speaking the language;
- Prior education disrupted by war;
- Illiteracy, even in the mother tongue;
- Bullying and/or the first experiences of racism; and
- Low expectations and lack of sympathy or empathy on the part of teachers – *"cruelty from teachers."*

---

[8] The Refugee Youth Work Forum is an emerging organisation. The idea for such a group came from a number of refugee youth workers, after completing training, stating that they wished to meet on a continuing basis to discuss common issues.

The need for *"a welcoming atmosphere, love and security"* in school as well as additional language and educational support was highlighted. Without these, students are likely to feel angry and hopeless and to lose self-confidence. These feelings in turn can result in difficult behaviour and resultant marginalisation or even exclusion from the school.

> *"They arrive here from refugee camps and are put in a class with their peers; they don't speak English, they become disruptive, they're bullied and they often fight back."* (See also: Somali Youth Development Project Annual Report, Acton, 1996 and *Invisible Students*, Children of the Storm, 1998.)

Many young refugees struggle with their memories of life in their home country. They may have left behind a very comfortable lifestyle, having highly educated parents with high expectations, a good school and a good home; they may have left family members and friends behind; they may have been sent ahead; they may have been witness to atrocity, to hate and anger.

> *"We were packed up as two sisters. There was a war on, and as women we were in danger of rape or murder. We left everyone else behind and had to cope on our own."*

Participants discussed evidence of a high level of unaddressed anger among young refugees, due to their experiences and their losses. These are often expressed in withdrawal, rebellious behaviour, rejection and truancy, as well as in other symptoms like bed-wetting.

Participants talked at length of what Mohamoud Aden (1996) calls 'cross cultural shock'. This describes young refugees operating at the interface between their family culture and that of the host country. The refugee youth workers called this the *"day time and night time culture – they have two personalities, sometimes, even two sets of clothes."* This 'cross cultural shock' has the potential to alienate young people from parents and/or elders in their communities.

As the young people pick up the language, culture and knowledge of the systems here, their parents become increasingly dependent on them, using them as interpreters and guides. At the same time the parents' self esteem falls. They try to bring up their children as they would at home.

> *"Conflict is high."*
> *"They have to steer a dangerous path."*

Addressing the Issues

The group proposed a number of strategies. Participants emphasised the value and potential of supplementary schools to provide an important link between young people and families and help to identify problems and issues arising for young people. Supplementary schools can also, of course, address some of the issues arising from disrupted education. They also identified a number of weaknesses in supplementary schooling:

- there is often a lack of physical space to hold classes;
- classes often hold very high numbers [as reported in the RCO question-naire responses] with a wide age range. Attention and individual support are often insufficient in these large mixed classes;
- most schools depend on volunteers [again borne out in the RCO question-naire responses] and need more experienced and qualified teachers;
- most lack appropriate teaching materials and aids; and
- there are few links between supplementary schools and mainstream educational provision. Links with the young people's own schools are needed.

Simply put, supplementary schools need more resources.

Participants felt that good youth workers were essential to provide role models for young people and to develop empathetic relationships. They felt that these youth workers need to be younger adults who have begun the process of their own integration into this society so that they can act as crucial bridges between the younger and older generations in a community.

Participants also stressed the importance of refugee youth workers' relationships with parents and elders in a community. The refugee youth worker's role was seen as including:

- communication with parents;
- acting as advocate for young people;
- helping parents to understand; and
- reassuring parents.

They stated that the role of a youth worker is not understood by most parents, as they traditionally try to keep problem solving within the family. Youth workers need to make themselves approachable to parents and build relationships of trust. Most important, confidentiality to both parents and young people must be respected.

Many young refugees need to interact with a wide range of statutory services: schools, colleges, careers services, educational welfare, employment and training agencies and health and social services. These frequently do not demonstrate understanding of the complexities of their users' lives. The young people need knowledgeable adult advocates to facilitate and empower them in these interactions, and, of course, the agencies need to develop awareness in their responses.

Generational Conflict: Discussion

A key issue for the RCO coordinators and for the refugee youth workers was inter-generational conflict. However it was not a major issue for the young refugees we interviewed in Section 2. Why this seeming contradiction?

Some of the explanation for this discrepancy is one of organisation. Different members of the research team were responsible for the reports on these different parts of the study. The timetable for the study meant that the interviews with young refugees (Section 2) were completed by the time the results of the interviews with coordinators were available. No explicit questions were raised with young refugees asking about conflict with parents and elders. However, there were parts of the interview where respondents were asked questions that gave some indications on this question.

When young refugees were asked about activities, a number indicated that they wanted a much broader provision than was being provided. More to the point, the interviewers raised for discussion with young refugees a number of topics concerning how respondents saw their future. These questions asked where interviewees expected to be living in five to ten years time; and if they were to marry, where did they think their partner would come from? There were also questions about what language they thought they would bring up any children to use, and what their links were likely to be with their country of origin.

The answers aroused much interest within the groups but did not always work with all groups (especially the younger ones). The discussions exposed differences in some groups with a few of the older women making it clear that they did not want to marry anyone from their own cultural background. There were some indications that a number of the young people were moving away from identity with their communities towards a more British/English or more Westernised identity. This last point should be seen as an impression, not a firm conclusion.

This question about the future was not analysed mainly because it did not work for all groups and we had (and still have) doubts about the accuracy of any responses. Additionally, the section was already overlong, concentrating on harder information.

However, this only partly explains the discrepancy between the two sets of responses. While there were no explicit questions asked about generational conflict, it is clear that it was not the first topic in the young people's minds. So why was there so little mention of inter-generational conflict?

First, for four groups interviewed it was hardly an issue. Two groups (the Kosovan and Iranian) lived in hostels with no family in the UK; and in two groups, the AYA (Kosovan) and Algerian, only one of the group lived with a member of their family. Examination for conflict should therefore focus on the five groups (Armenian, School, Somali, Ugandan and Vietnamese), nearly all of whom lived with members of their families.

Four of these five groups were interviewed in community centres/youth projects which were part of their community structure. It seems a fair conclusion that those young people most alienated from their own communities (or the communities of their parents) are unlikely to attend such provision. In that sense, we interviewed a sample which by definition would not include a fair representation of the most alienated, or to put it another way those most integrated/attracted to a British way of life. For the majority we interviewed, especially the younger ones, their attendance almost certainly is with the approval of parents/elder relatives and they are more likely to be 'less problematical' to their communities.

Allowing for the fact that those interviewed were not likely to be the main focus of their elders' anxiety over generational conflict, there were still signs of potential conflict. Many of the young people talked about wanting to have 'fun'. Quite where are the boundaries of 'acceptable fun' and 'unacceptable behaviour' is obviously a moot question. A number of young women and girls commented on the activities open to them. The wish to go swimming, have trips out, etc. could cut across more traditional attitudes. As one young woman, born in the UK, said, in her community sexism was alive and well even if it was inappropriate in the UK.

Despite the reasons for this discrepancy in this study, it is still our conclusion that the inadequacies of youth provision has much more to do with lack of resources and suitable premises and staff, than to do with cultural resistance by refugee communities. That there is an inter-generational clash of values is something we see as inevitable; it is part of the history of literally every migrant group to a new society. However, despite the fears of those responsible for refugee community organisations, we do not think it is quite the same overwhelming problem seen from the perspective of many of the young.

We expect the current generations of young refugees to negotiate the demands between two cultures with many of the skills that earlier waves of immigrants to the UK have used. Some will do it better, some will do it worse; some will accommodate to one culture and reject the other. Some will retain the love, trust and respect of their elders, and some will not. The flexibility and adaptability of the elders of communities will be a crucial factor.

Consulting with Refugee Communities: Findings

- Refugee community organisations are **the principal providers of youth work** for young refugees in London. Seventy seven per cent of the organisations in our sample were providing some kind of support and activity, seemingly to more than 3,000 young refugees in London.

- The experience of asylum seeking and the events which lead to it can generate a range of deeply complex dynamics. These affect the personal and social development of young people, their families and communities. Many younger adults in these communities have experienced these issues and developed strategies for addressing them. As such they may provide a 'bridge' between the generations. Therefore, the development of youth work and youth workers should be viewed as an essential.

- However, almost all refugee community organisations stated that their work with young refugees is severely under-resourced in terms of finance, staffing and training. This is borne out by the high level of volunteering in these organisations, against the very low level of qualification for youth work.

- Training for those working with, or wishing to develop work with, young people in the community context is clearly a priority.

- Refugee community organisations need the backing of mainstream services and funders, not simply for grant aid but in the provision of access to resources, equipment, materials and activities in the wider community.

- For some young refugees, for example those experiencing post-traumatic stress, back up referral services are essential.

- Young refugees often need to interact with a wider range of statutory agencies than most young people. Liaison with schools, colleges, careers services, educational welfare, social services, immigration services, employment and training services is an integral and important element in the role of the youth worker working with young refugees.

- These agencies need training and awareness raising to perform their role effectively and sympathetically.

- The absolute necessity of working with the parents and families of young refugees has been highlighted, and liaison should be recognised as a crucial element of the youth worker's role. Parenting projects for refugees, tailored for different cultural/national groups, should be considered.

Section Four:

MAINSTREAM YOUTH WORK PROVISION

In this section, mainstream youth work providers are defined as "any organisations in the statutory or voluntary youth sectors that are not refugee led".

The Policy Context – General

Before examining mainstream youth work provision in Greater London, it is necessary to briefly examine the policy context in which youth work for refugees and asylum-seekers exists. Despite the debate that has raged, and continues to rage about refugees, immigration control, and 'bogus' asylum seekers, there is a curious vacuum. Few policies actually govern British society's responsibilities to asylum seekers once they arrive here. Government has failed to take the lead in developing policies for the social integration of asylum seekers and those who have been given leave to stay. It has generally been left to the main institutions of British society to work out what to do with the children and adults who have arrived. The gaps left by public services have been mainly filled by charities and by voluntary and community organisations, often with little assistance from mainstream services.

Evidence of this absence of detailed policy debate and leadership can easily be found in official papers. For example, in April 2000 the Social Exclusion Unit published *A National Strategy for Neighbourhood Renewal: a framework for consultation*. In a 130-page document focusing on the most deprived neighbourhoods in England, not a single mention is to be found of refugees or asylum seekers. This document is based on 18 Policy Action Team reports, totalling over 1,500 pages and more than 600 recommendations, but refugees and asylum seekers are conspicuous by their absence.[9] What makes their absence even more strange is that the areas focused on in the

---

[9] The 18 Policy Action Team (PATs) reports are summarised in *Policy Action Team report summaries: a compendium*, available from Social Exclusion Unit, April 2000. PAT1 (Jobs for All) does devote half a page (p62) to an example of work with refugees and one minor recommendation (not important enough to be included in the summary volume).

National Strategy for Neighbourhood Renewal are exactly those in which the vast bulk of asylum seekers have settled in the past, i.e. before the policies for dispersal started being implemented in 1999. Additionally, many of these areas are likely to be those receiving refugees and asylum seekers under the new dispersal policies. So we must ask; what explains their absence?

The problem lies at the heart of government. The lead department for all matters dealing with refugees and asylum seekers is the Immigration and Nationality Division (IND) of the Home Office. The IND is dominated by political imperatives around refugees such as control, dispersal, etc. Long term developmental questions come, not unnaturally, a poor second. When IND issued a consultation paper on *The Integration of Recognised Refugees* in October 1999 it was in response to the fierce reactions of local authorities and other public services to proposed dispersal policies[10]. Previously, the steady build up of refugees over many years had been mainly concentrated in Greater London areas long used to absorbing immigrants from almost every country in the world. Dispersal policies placing refugees in areas unused to immigrants and populations of different racial and cultural backgrounds created backlashes. As the responsible government department, IND had to create the semblance of policies.

Examination of the proposed policies suggests a lack of detailed thinking on the matter. The role of refugee community organisations is vague and it is clear that there is very little understanding of any of the principles of community development. This document appeared at the same time that another part of the Home Office (the Active Community Unit) was issuing a detailed report on Community Self-Help[11]. It would be ironic if it were not so sad. No mention whatsoever is made of any youth provision in the IND consultation.

The IND recognises that a high proportion of past asylum seekers has been given leave to stay and that the proportion is unlikely to fall to any great extent. It recognises that the integration of those given leave to remain in the UK is of the highest importance. Yet it fails to recognise the need to provide services for some of the most vulnerable of an extremely vulnerable group – young people, many of them without their families, far from home and all they know.

The department responsible for Youth Services, the Department for Education and Employment (DfEE), has followed the lead of the IND. In a period when the DfEE (and the Social Exclusion Unit) have issued a number of reports on the

[10] *A Consultation Paper on the Integration of Recognised Refugees in the UK,* Home Office, Immigration & Nationality Division, October 1999.
[11] *Report of the Policy Action Team on Community Self-Help,* available from Active Community Unit, Home Office, September 1999.

position of young people and specifically on the future shape of the Youth Service and the proposed Youth Support Scheme, there is no mention of young refugees or asylum seekers.[12] The DfEE (or its predecessor departments) have never issued any circulars or advice to local education authorities (LEAs) on youth services for young refugees.

Over the last 10 to 15 years, the Youth Service has been under great pressure. LEAs facing budgetary pressures have continually cut Youth Service provision in order to maintain statutory services. The DfEE has until very recently (after the fieldwork for this study was completed), shown very little interest in Youth Service and given no lead about developments.[13] It is therefore not surprising that the development of youth services for this most vulnerable of groups has been patchy, to say the least. Where LEAs have had to make cuts, communities with more political clout are most likely to come off best. By definition refugees are among the least powerful groups in society.

A common assumption, at national level, further explains this policy vacuum. After many years of struggle, policies and monitoring for black and minority ethnic groups have been established in most areas – and all the documents cited in this section refer frequently to black and minority ethnic groups. It has been a common assumption that where such policies have been established, they cover refugees and asylum seekers. The test of this assumption is whether it does, in fact, deliver to refugees and asylum seekers and their organisations[14].

The Policy Context – Some Implications of Dispersal

This study has focused on the youth work needs of young refugees in Greater London. Up until 1999, this meant that the study was covering 85 per cent of all refugees in the UK. The overwhelming majority of refugees and asylum seekers were

---

[12] *Connexions: The best start in life for every young person*, DfEE, January, 2000. A number of other recent reports from the DfEE and Social Exclusion Unit have also failed to discuss these issues – these include: Policy Action Team report 11, *Schools Plus*, DfEE, 2000; Policy Action Team report 12, *Young People*, SEU, 2000; *Bringing Britain Together*, SEU, 1999; *Learning to Succeed*, DfEE, 1999.

[13] At the time of writing two major proposals likely to affect provision of youth work services are out for consultation. These are the *Connexions* strategy (ibid.) with proposals for a Youth Support Scheme, and the *National Strategy for Neighbourhood Renewal* (op cit.), Key Idea 26 for a cross-departmental Ministerial group on youth issues, with better local coordination.

[14] In June 2000 the Social Exclusion Unit issued, *Minority Ethnic Issues in Social Exclusion and Neighbourhood Renewal*, as part of the National Strategy for Neighbourhood Renewal. This document brings together all the findings and recommendations of all the Policy Action Teams. It fails to mention refugees or asylum seekers.

concentrated in the Greater London area. However, the 1999 Immigration and Asylum Act could well change this situation.

In anticipation of the Act, dispersal policies have now been in operation since mid 1999 for the majority of new asylum seekers; this is in addition to the arrangements that were made for asylum seekers at the time of the war in Kosova. This means that the issues we have been discussing in this study are now likely to confront many local authorities throughout the country.

The intention of the Act is: *"to relieve the pressure on the local authorities, central government services and communities in London and the South East and provide coherent support for asylum seekers in the dispersal areas . . . This dispersal policy has implications for the host communities, where the newly arrived refugees will be settled, and makes the coordination and development of effective integration policies increasingly important. Integration is not only essential for the refugees themselves, but also in the wider context of the Government's policies on social inclusion generally, community and race relations."* (Home Office 1999)

The priorities are clear from this statement. It is about relieving pressure on the areas carrying 'the greatest burdens' [15]. It is not about the ability of host areas to meet the specific needs of refugees and asylum seekers. It is not about where the integration of refugees would be enhanced. It is not about the economic and social vitality of areas of reception.

Many of these authorities will be facing a new situation. While many of these authorities will have been used to dealing over many years with an increasing multi-ethnic population, the movement of refugees and asylum seekers will be a new experience.

A number of factors need to be considered. The first is the type of area to which refugees and asylum seekers will be dispersed. It is likely that many of the areas will be areas of unpopular housing with many current vacancies in housing stock. These are likely, therefore, to be areas with low economic vitality with more than their fair share of modern urban problems. Problems of crime are likely to be common. In this situation, refugees and asylum seekers could easily become scapegoats and targets for racial harassment. Young people are among the most vulnerable and local police, youth workers and other authorities will need to be extra alert to these problems.

A second factor is that in most of these areas it is likely that there will be no community of earlier arrivals to smooth the path for more recent arrivals. This can be

[15] It is of interest to note that the concentrations of refugees and asylum seekers in a number of London boroughs have been for many years far greater than current levels in the very well publicised concentrations in certain Kent towns.

seen by examination of the most comprehensive directory of refugee resources: *Refugee Resources in the UK, 1999*. In this directory, 172 pages are needed to list community organisations, legal advisors, Racial Equality Councils, voluntary organisations and others who provide services for refugees in London, (the majority being community organisations). For the rest of the UK, including Northern Ireland, Scotland and Wales, only 75 pages are required to list all relevant organisations (the biggest group being semi–official bodies with community organisations being a minority).[16]

Our study has shown that one of the biggest sources of support for young refugees and their families are members of their own community. In Greater London, refugee community organisations are much more highly concentrated than anywhere else in the country. It seems unlikely that their role in supporting the newly arrived can be replicated by the normal statutory and voluntary services as envisaged by the IND consultation document. This means that local youth services will have to take initiatives and be imaginative in the solutions that they develop.

The third factor is well put by the following:

Minority ethnic communities experience a double disadvantage. They are disproportionately concentrated in deprived areas and experience all the problems that affect other people in these areas. But people from minority ethnic communities also suffer the consequences of racial discrimination; services that fail to reach them or meet their needs; and language and cultural barriers in gaining access to information and services. (SEU, 1999c), p8.

We do not disagree with that assessment, but note that, if minority ethnic communities suffer a double disadvantage, then refugee communities suffer similar but even greater disadvantage. Much of that additional disadvantage local authorities and services, including the Youth Service, can do little about. One cannot change the history, experiences and traumas that so many asylum seekers have had. However, their current 'invisibility' when services are planned can be rectified. Youth services have a major role to play.

The final factor is that in many of these areas, local authorities and Youth Service providers start with a clean sheet. They will not have the history that both assists and

---

[16] *Refugee Resources in the UK, 1999*, pub Refugee Council, 1999. The directory, while not totally comprehensive, is the best source available on refugee organisations and services. The contrast between the number of community organisations in London and the rest of the country is startling. Thus both of the adjoining London boroughs of Camden and Islington each have more refugee organisations than any major conurbation in the rest of the UK or in Northern Ireland, Scotland and Wales combined.

besets providers in areas like London. The Youth Service, like other services, will be able to take new initiatives and experiment with ideas. The task will be to channel and encourage the energy and strengths that so many refugees possess.

Many of the receiving authorities in run down areas see the dispersal of asylum seekers to their locality as yet another burden. Ironically, if they can be positive the presence of new, able and energetic people may be a great opportunity. They need to remember that that many of the refugees who were such burdens in the 1930s, the 1960s and the 1970s (Jews, East African Asians and Cypriots) are now seen as very positive contributors to British culture, society and the economy.

Local Authority Youth Services

All 33 Greater London Boroughs were sent a questionnaire asking for information on their policies, if any, towards young refugees. They were also asked to detail all projects in their area catering for young refugees. The questionnaire asked for details of all youth work provision and additionally for other services that might come under the aegis of the Youth Service such as play, supplementary education, etc. Finally questions were asked relating to a number of topics with reference to young refugees such as budgets, training policies, numbers of staff with direct responsibility for work with young refugees, and the numbers of refugees employed by the Service.

Questionnaires were sent to the Youth Service of each borough. In some instances, where Youth Service responsibilities were incorporated within another departmental title (such as Play, Recreation or Community Education), questionnaires were sent to that department. The questionnaires were addressed to the senior person responsible for Youth Service as identified by the National Youth Agency (NYA) list of all local authority youth services. In one case where the borough youth service had been contracted out to a number of providers, questionnaires were sent to each provider, (the responses being treated as a single response in this section).

Response was slow and reminder letters with copy questionnaires were sent out a month after the initial questionnaires. In total, 13 questionnaires were returned. The following analysis refers to these 13 responses. A response rate of 42 per cent is quite good for a postal questionnaire. Those who responded included a number of London boroughs where one would expect high concentrations of refugees and some where expectations would be for lower concentrations. There is no reason to regard the results of this survey as unrepresentative. Differences may exist in non-responding boroughs but it is unlikely to be in the direction of greater youth work activity than in those which responded.

The reported extent of youth work provision for refugees was low in the sample responding. In fact it was low for all work with young refugees. Two respondents gave 'nil' returns. Others, where one may have expected considerable activity, gave low returns, often stating that there was general provision and young refugees, like everyone else, could access this provision. From evidence gathered from other sources, it seems that in some cases youth officers/youth work managers (who were in the main completing the questionnaires) were not always aware of what was going on at ground level in the clubs and projects for which they were responsible.

Issues

All respondents were asked the series of questions listed below. We include a brief analysis of the responses and highlight any interpretation.

1. Does your authority have any specific policies regarding youth services for young refugees?

None of the respondent authorities has any specific policies with regard to young refugees. One respondent reported that the authority had "ethnic cultures as one of its priorities." A second stated that it had no policy, had not thought about it and maybe it should.

2. Are there any specific ways in which the authority supports work with young refugees?

a) Direct budget allocation? Two answered Yes to this question. One reported a £91,000 budget allocation jointly funded by the local authority and the DfEE. The second reported that it funded one worker to work with refugees as part of a fuller brief. One authority stated 'No', but qualified their answer by stating that they do allocate funds to refugee projects.

b) Staff development and training? Six respondents claimed to provide for refugees in training. In a sense though, they indicated that training for refugees and work with refugees was part of their generic staff development and that people could or could not participate as applicable. There was little sense that refugees had special needs and may need specific encouragement. Two local authorities commented that they offer one session on working with refugees within their general introductory training.

c) Rights and representation of refugees? Three authorities mentioned moves in this direction. In two cases they specifically talked of representation on the local Youth Council, and in one case of facilitating representation on the Youth Council.

d) Any other policies re. refugees? Five authorities mentioned actions under this heading. One referred to young refugees' use of mainstream provision. Another stated that the authority gives grant aid to voluntary organisations, and while refugee organisations were not specifically targeted they were encouraged to apply. One authority stated that it gave support (not specified) to local Somali, Turkish and Kurdish groups. Another mentioned that an inter-departmental focus group was being developed and the needs of young refugees would be met by this group. Finally, one authority stated that a part-time youth worker represented the Service on the Borough Homelessness Group, and that that worker also picked up the needs of young refugees.

3. Does your authority employ any workers, full or part-time, with specific responsibilities for young refugees?

Four authorities reported employing staff with specific responsibilities. One authority employs two part-time workers seconded to a Vietnamese refugee association. One authority employs five fractional youth workers and two tutors (all Somalis) who work with a Somali association. One authority employs a full-time senior youth worker, four part-time workers and five peripatetic tutors to work solely with refugees in the borough. Finally, one authority employs an area team leader whose brief is to support voluntary groups within specific communities, and an Asian development worker to enable young people from Asian communities to access mainstream provision and facilitate development of community based provision.

4. Does your authority employ any workers, full or part-time, who were refugees?

All of the workers described in the first three authorities in the above paragraph were themselves refugees, except for two part-time workers in the third authority. Neither of the two workers described for the fourth authority were refugees, but the authority stated that it was employing a part-time Somali trainee for informal work with young men. A fifth authority stated that it was about to employ both a Kosovan and a Kurdish youth worker.

Discussion

No Youth Service respondents had specific policies with regard to young refugees. A number of authorities believed that policies prioritising ethnic minorities cover young refugees.

All refugee workers, with one exception, were part-time, generally of low status or had responsibility for refugees only as part of a much wider brief. Only one authority had a senior youth worker (with a recognised professional qualification) who actually was a refugee and supervised other staff.

Two authorities reported development of borough wide policies for refugees and that the Youth Service was involved in the discussion. It is possible that many more authorities are developing such policies and that Youth Services are not involved.

Overall, this insight into London borough Youth Service reaction to the presence of young refugees suggests many organisational deficiencies and lack of information about what is happening on the ground.[17]

Youth Work 'Umbrella' Organisations

We sent seven questionnaires to a selection of the larger, voluntary 'umbrella' youth work organisations and received six responses.[18] We asked for information about organisational policies, budgets, staff development, rights and representation, activities and staffing in relation to youth work with young refugees.

Two of these organisations support a membership of local youth clubs and projects in Greater London. One works similarly but within a particular faith group and at national level. The fourth is a national organisation promoting and franchising a scheme for young people aimed at their personal development. The remaining two have a national brief to represent and serve as advocate for young people nationally.

Taking each category of organisation in turn:

There were two 'membership' organisations: the first has a membership of 150 youth groups with a brief to 'extend the scope of youth work and work with children in the Greater London area.' This organisation gave a 'nil' response to all questions with the added comment: "No specific work being developed or in progress for young refugees."

The second organisation has a remit to "give young people access to a range of learning opportunities and challenging experiences which promote their personal and social development." It has three refugee community organisations in a membership of 500 youth clubs and projects, (all three RCOs have contributed to this research). This organisation does not have specific policies or budget allocations for youth work with young refugees. It does state that it is looking at its training

---

[17] See below in this section 'Dialogue with mainstream youth workers', for evidence that some Youth Service responses were unaware of local developments/work.

[18] The questionnaires to youth work 'umbrellas' and those to voluntary organisations (see following part of this section) were very similar to the questionnaires to local authority Youth Services.

programme "with a view to the future," although it does not elaborate. No staff members are refugees or have responsibility for working with young refugees but it stated that many of its member groups "work in ethnic minority areas."

The faith-based organisation gave a 'nil' response to all questions stating: "Our organisation does not specifically deal with refugees as a group".

The fourth organisation franchises a personal development programme for young people. It also gave a 'nil' response to all questions. However, a covering letter stated:

> "Refugees may be participating ... but unfortunately we are not aware of it and as the programme is franchised to other organisations it would be hard to determine if there were any. We have not given sufficient thought to involving young people from this background and I am not aware of any specific initiatives, but your letter has prompted us to review the situation. Thank you very much for bringing this important matter to our attention."

Of the two organisations with a remit to represent and advocate for young people, one provided evidence of policy formulation in advocating for refugees. Both stated that their approach is achieved through general advocacy and research. One stated that it had no young refugees in membership although young refugees were included in its statistical fact sheets.

None of these six organisations employ staff with responsibility for young refugees' issues or have refugee employees.

On the basis of these six responses, it may be safe to assume that, as with the local authority Youth Services, organisations which have a specific brief to promote and support the development of youth work in London are doing little to provide specifically for young refugees. Once again we see evidence of young refugees being subsumed within the overall category of 'ethnic minority'.

Consulting Voluntary Organisations

Twenty-three questionnaires were sent to a selection of the larger mainstream (non-refugee led) voluntary organisations which have either remits to work with refugees or to work with children and young people. We received eight responses, four from organisations with specific remits to work with refugees and asylum seekers, and four from organisations with general remits, e.g. 'to combat poverty' or to 'provide services for children and young people.'

We asked these organisations for information about their organisational policies, budgets, staff development, rights and representation, activities and staffing in relation to work with young refugees.

Organisations Working with Refugees

Each of the four responding organisations is different. One is a national agency providing therapeutic services and support for refugees from 72 different countries. This agency is a key resource and referral agency for organisations working with refugee children and young people. It also publishes material with specific reference to young refugees and employs a diverse range of staff and volunteers in its work.

The second organisation provides assistance to asylum seekers on all aspects of immigration. It gave a 'nil' response to all questions relating to young refugees, but stated: "We would be happy to train young refugees as volunteer advice workers".

The third is a refugee housing organisation which as part of its wider services, provides supported housing for unaccompanied young refugees. It gave a 'nil' response to all other questions.

The fourth has a UK remit to support the educational needs of young refugees and is primarily concerned with supporting children and young people in schools. It also publishes material aimed at teachers and others concerned with educational support for young refugees. It is not clear whether it employs paid or voluntary staff in its work, as the organisation simply stated that it does not employ staff with specific responsibilities for young refugees nor does it directly employ refugees.

Generic Voluntary Organisations

Of the four generic organisations, two are large organisations working in the field of homelessness while two are large children's charities. The first homelessness organisation gave a 'nil' response to all questions.

The second provided a very broad based service to young homeless people: "Housing, support, and care including access to employment, training and education" as well as "providing support to voluntary groups and local authorities nationally to develop strategies for meeting the housing needs of young people". Although it has no specific policy, budget allocation or staff development programme to support its work with young refugees, this organisation stated that it does work with young refugees and asylum seekers "on an individual basis, clearly trying to match needs and aspirations through our generic service provision. We access specific services, e.g. interpreters, the Medical Foundation for the Victims of Torture, specialist housing provision – but based on the needs of individuals – to work with each young person we house."

In addition to its range of generic services accessed by young refugees, this organisation also works in partnership to support at least one specific housing service for young refugees. In this project, refugee workers are employed. It was unable to provide information regarding the employment of refugees as it "does not monitor from this perspective".

Although neither of the two remaining organisations provides youth work with young refugees, both provide specific direct services for young refugees through individual local projects. The first does this through its Refugee Scheme in one south London borough, employing three workers. Whilst the organisation states that it does not have specific policies regarding services for young refugees, it also states that it advocates for young refugees through its various projects.

The second organisation provides specific services for young refugees through its 'Rights and Participation Project' for young people who are 'looked after' (in the care of a local authority) in three south and east London boroughs.

This Project provides Independent Visitors (IVs) for unaccompanied 'looked after' young refugees. It advocates through working with the local authority's social services to develop policy in relation to young refugees, e.g. to ensure that young asylum seekers' status is clarified before they reach the age of 18 years [and thus 'leave care']. The project employs an IV coordinator and engages refugees as volunteer IVs.

This was the only organisation that cited staff development and training *"through working with Victims of Torture"*. It also stated that it belongs to a voluntary sector consortium *"concerned to improve policy and practice for young refugees."*

These responses clearly show the potential for developing mainstream work for refugees. Where the work is happening, each project is different, each focused in some way towards specific aspects of young refugees' issues and needs, and each is able to articulate the work and (in some cases) publish it.

Dialogue with Mainstream Youth Workers

Twenty-five non-refugee youth workers in mainstream youth work projects were randomly selected and invited to attend a consultation/training day to discuss their perspectives on youth work with young refugees. Of the seven who accepted the invitation, four were senior youth workers responsible for either local authority youth projects [3] or youth projects in voluntary organisations [1]. One was a youth worker in a voluntary organisation with a brief to develop work with young Somalis in a local area. One works in her authority's Youth Service training department. These workers all came from two inner London boroughs. The Youth Service in one of these boroughs had responded to our questionnaire.

On the day, participants explored their perspectives on the experiences and impact on families and communities of the asylum seeking process, the consequent issues in young refugees' lives here in London, and the possible range of responses which youth work could make. Dialogue and discussion were facilitated by a trainer who is herself a refugee.

Some of the conclusions for mainstream youth workers were:

- a need to encourage and facilitate refugees to engage in youth work;
- to explore ways of making resources and facilities which they manage available to refugee communities;
- to recognise and target young refugees' communities as they do with other communities;
- to recognise that young refugees have multiple needs, like all other young people, as well as to engage with their refugee status; and
- to recognise the fine line between collusion and empowerment in working with refugee communities.

All the participants stated that the day had been of value, and that more training around this issue would be useful

Youth workers in this group reported initiatives in their boroughs for working with young refugees. These initiatives took place within the local authority Youth Service or were grant aided by the Youth Service. This information was not provided to us through the local authority questionnaires and we think it significant that the local youth office did not refer to the detail of work in progress.[19]

Consulting Mainstream Youth Services: Findings

- Young refugees are not visible in mainstream Youth Services. There is an evident lack of awareness and understanding of the specific needs of young refugees in local authority Youth Services and the large voluntary youth

[19] In addition to this example, we gathered in the course of research two other examples where local Youth Services failed to report projects in their area.

work organisations where, at best, young refugees seem to be subsumed within the larger category of 'ethnic minority.' There was little evidence of policy or strategic planning for working with young refugees. Awareness raising activity is clearly needed to free up access to the many (often under-used) physical and human resources available.

- If this is the case in London, which has a relatively high proportion of refugees in its population and a developed refugee community sector, it is likely that Youth Services nationally will be in a similar position. The implications of dispersal in the current Asylum Act suggest that a national awareness programme is needed.

- The support function of the large 'umbrella' youth work organisations could be utilised to enable RCOs to access resources and networks in the Youth Service as a whole.

- Most examples of good practice were to be found in the voluntary sector where the work was focused at project level, and readily articulated. However, given the size of this sector (some of Britain's largest charities work for children and young people) one may have expected to see more evidence of the development of this work.

- Tentative signs of increased activity in Youth Services were seen at the time of the recent Kosovan crisis. On the evidence of this research, Youth Services will need to give deep consideration to how new posts are developed and managed. Specific consideration needs to be given to Youth Services' relationships with the refugee community sector. Partnerships, joint working, and shared resources are likely to be crucial to the effectiveness of these new initiatives.

Section Five:

EXAMPLES OF YOUTH WORK WITH YOUNG REFUGEES

This section of the research report provides 'snapshots' of youth work with young refugees in London. In this we hope to explore:

- further perceptions of the youth work needs of young refugees;
- some of the many ways in which effective youth work with young refugees can develop in different organisational contexts; and
- some of the issues raised through the work.

We visited four youth work projects, selected to offer contrast in type of provision and organisational context.

Interview One: The Centre for Armenian Information and Advice (CAIA)

CAIA is a refugee community organisation based in West London and serving the Armenian community across London and nationally through its web site and newsletter. Established in 1986, the organisation states its aims as follows:

> "The Centre for Armenian Information and Advice seeks to enhance the quality of life for disadvantaged members of the Armenian community in London, specifically those in poverty, isolation and distress. We support their diverse needs through the provision of welfare, education and cultural services at a welcoming centre for all Armenians."

Operating from its building in Acton, the organisation offers immediate help to recently arrived asylum seekers from parts of the former Soviet Union, Iraq and Iran. In its welfare, education and cultural programme, the oldest and youngest members of the community are its highest priority. Since its inception, it has offered an under-

5s playgroup and a summer play-scheme for school age children. It has long since tried to develop work with the older children and young people, and in 1995 it piloted a social club for this age group. It won funding from BBC Children in Need in 1999 to develop its youth work programme.

CAIA employed a youth worker and started its youth club in 1999. The RCO coordinator and the full-time youth worker were interviewed.

The youth club meets on Friday evenings and has a membership of 142 young people, a mailing list of 250 families and a steady weekly attendance of 40 or so young people aged between 10 and 18 years. Because of the shortage of experienced workers, the coordinator works alongside the youth worker in the youth club with the assistance of a group of the older teenagers – mainly student volunteers – and some parents who also volunteer, e.g. providing food for events.

Activities are planned and publicised in advance. Over the last ten months these have included Armenian cultural and history events, drama workshops, workshops on bullying and racial harassment (in conjunction with a range of external agencies), a fashion show, line dancing, a science and palaeontology workshop, a bring and buy sale, discos, a 'blind date' evening, table tennis tournament, Armenian TV and a non-alcoholic cocktail party.

Many of these activities are led by visiting members of the Armenian community, e.g. from the Armenian Church, the Natural History Museum and the Armenian Table Tennis Club as well as two professional actors who have run workshops and offered to do this on an ongoing basis subject to resources.

The programme of activity is well documented with reports and photographs as well as the monthly programme, which is mailed out to all on the list. The Armenian Voice, the organisation's newsletter, reports these experiences:

"Opportunities to be involved in diverse workshops, meet interesting people and enjoy the friendly environment . . . full of fun and music . . . a memorable evening . . . touched the hearts of the young people with expectation, fun and love . . . curious and interested young people gathered around . . . happy and excited teenagers . . . experimented late into the evening." [20]

This is the first youth work of its kind in the Armenian community. In the worker's own words:

[20] Armenian Voice, newsletter for the London Armenian community, Winter 2000. Published by CAIA

"We are learning how to develop it. We welcome the parents' support but also recognise that young people need time on their own. We need professional advice and support and training to help us develop our staff and volunteers. We feel that we are developing this alone. We feel limited in many of the things we can do because we have yet to develop the staff team. So, for example, it is really difficult to take young people off-site for activities because we do not have enough staff to leave behind."

However, the organisation has received little assistance from the local Youth Service:

"We approached the local Youth Service when we first got the grant and asked for support. We wanted professional advice, access to youth work networks, and perhaps someone to sit on our support group, and maybe to work alongside of us. We asked for someone to come along and see us, help us to explore the needs of our staff and young people. An officer did come along one evening . . . We got a £250 grant from the service for equipment. Apart from occasionally inviting us to meetings nothing more has been offered. So, for the moment we've given up on the borough."

The two workers expressed an urgent need for training and staff development:

"We need training. We've finally negotiated a course for the youth worker, but now we're having difficulty getting a supervisor for her. We are also joining in with Action Acton's youth work training this summer. Funders have been quite responsive with equipment grants. Now that we've managed to develop some training we hope to settle down and get to grips with it. It's trial and error — we started cold and are working it out as we go along. We would like the kind of support that a qualified youth worker could offer, guidance and someone on our support group. We need someone who could look at the work from the outside and help us to develop confidence to develop it ourselves."

Interview Two: The Lambeth Young Refugees Development Project

This is a project of the London Borough of Lambeth Youth Service, established in 1991 through DfEE Section 210 funding. The project mainly works with young people who are living in Lambeth's many hostels. The Project's stated aims are:

"To combat loneliness, build confidence and ease young refugees' integration into the

wider community. It does this through a broad programme of social and cultural education including advice and information, welfare rights, study skills, language support, recreational activities, sports, arts, outings and group work."

The Project has one full-time qualified senior youth worker, a refugee from Eritrea, and a team of part-time youth workers and tutors. Many of these are refugees.

We interviewed the full-time youth worker who has been in post since the inception of the Project. He is the only refugee with a nationally recognised youth work qualification that we encountered in this research study.

He discussed the early development of the Project. At first, he wanted to focus the Project's work on the provision of advice and information services but he recognised that such an approach would tie up his time and resources, focus only on the problematic areas of young refugees' lives and restrict his developmental role. During his time as a community and youth work student, he had undertaken a number of work placements through which he gained a vision of how youth work, within a community development approach, could be made to benefit young refugees.

"Young refugees share the dynamics and characteristics of all young people: they need to express themselves through music for instance; they need role models; they need to experiment; they need assistance towards independence and they need opportunities to lead."

He decided that a broader approach was needed:

"Under 18-year-olds had social workers, over 18s had nothing but a bed. Both needed more than what was being offered. They needed to be brought together, to develop relationships and support networks and be supported to take some ownership of their resettlement processes."

After a period of outreach work in the local hostels, the Project was launched with a high profile social and cultural evening at the town hall, followed by trips to the seaside, funfairs, ice rinks and bowling. Adult volunteers were recruited to work alongside part-time youth workers. Through these activities and the developing relationships, the Project could identify the young people's wider needs:

"for sport, art, advice and information, supplementary education, and a range of resettlement needs".

Mother tongue classes, supplementary education, art and sports were developed. By 1994, the Project was sponsoring four football teams and two basketball teams and taking trophies in the Lambeth Challenge Cup:

"These young refugees gained respect amongst wider groups of young people. All kinds of young people started to attend our social and cultural evenings. Evidence was developing that young refugees were being enabled to integrate into the wider Lambeth community."

Two rooms at one of the hostels were converted to art rooms, equipped by the Project, and tutors were engaged. Each summer between 1995 and 1997 a London FE college donated two full weeks of art tuition culminating in art exhibitions in Covent Garden.

"Art exposes the community and the young people. It gives expression to the young people and raises awareness in society."

During this time approximately ten young refugees from the project entered art school. Like many past members of the Project, many are still involved.

This work has become more urgent since the Project began:

"The status of young refugees has changed since the 1996 Asylum Act and continues to change with the most recent act. Hostels in Lambeth are occupied by young refugees existing without money – they get a bed and food and occasional bus fares for the doctor, the Immigration Office or for college, but otherwise they have no money at all. The hostels are a bit like a detention centre where they have to sign in and out. They are made to feel different from other young people. Life in the hostel can be very isolating, it slows their motivation and increases depression."

Project workers spend more time in the hostels. *"Just talking with them can be therapeutic"*. Through these discussions the young refugees often gain awareness of their needs and rights and this can lead them to be more demanding. The project has learned that it needs to work with the hostel workers, often before working with the young people, as this can make a difference to the young people's experience.

"We recently worked with two young Kosovans who were suicidal. They needed involvement in activities, in music, art, sport. They needed social lives. They needed competition. They needed an environment to work things through instead of being

isolated and lonely. They needed involvement and belongingness and someone to turn to. These are the things which can heal the trauma that they have so often experienced."

Whatever the Project provides for these young people, it has to resource 100 per cent. A very successful Eid party last February was attended by more than 100 young people drawn from a wide range of cultural backgrounds. Transport, food and music were provided by the Project:

"They want more of this. They need more of this. The Project needs the resources to provide more of this."

In the week preceding our follow up interview (in August 1999), the Project took 57 young refugees to Margate for the day in a coach and a minibus, accompanied by the senior worker and two fractional youth workers. All of these young people, who were from Kosova, the Horn of Africa, the Middle East, and Pakistan, reside in single sex hostels:

"Young men and women were brought together; food was taken along and shared; they experienced something of the British way of life; they were courageous, joining all the activities; barriers were broken down and relationships started to form; and of course, we discovered an emerging need – sexual health workshops will be organised in the Project over the coming months!"

In the week following our second interview, five young women refugees joined the Lambeth Young Women's Project's sailing and canoeing holiday in Devon. This is an achievement for both projects. The Refugee Project was able to engage in lengthy negotiation with the young women's families to gain their participation in the holiday, and the Young Women's Project extended its provision to young refugees – the two projects worked together.

"Mainstream projects could be doing so much more. But they need to work much harder to develop their links and gain the trust of families – the parents of these young women were very reluctant to let them go without the mediation I was able to offer."

Advice and information services have been integral to the work of the Project. In any one day, the youth workers may see four or five people seeking support and advice on immigration, education and health. The Project has active working relationships with a broad range of providers including social services, education welfare, legal advice centres, schools and refugee community organisations.

Supplementary schooling has offered education classes. Tutors have developed an approach focused on the demands and individual needs of the young people who are given lots of individual attention to build confidence, especially with language and study skills. Tutors are supported by youth workers who involve young people in a wide range of social education activities, encouraging and supporting them to come along, to understand their own needs, and to stretch themselves.

Interview Three: The Somali Refugee Development Project

This is a project in the London Borough of Ealing. The Project is funded by the LB of Ealing, with a Home Office Ethnic Minority Achievement Grant (EMAG) and European Social Fund (ESF) Objective 4. It is located in the LB of Ealing Education Department's Community Regeneration Unit and line managed by the community programme manager for 'Action Acton', a Single Regeneration Budget (SRB) funded regeneration programme for the South Acton estates. Established in 1995, the Project aims:

> "To address the needs of young Somali refugees aged between 15 and 25 years, living in and on the South Acton estate; to help them gain confidence and enhance self esteem; to enable them to reach the standard of education and skills necessary to access mainstream education, training and employment opportunities" (Project publicity, 1999).

The Project has one full-time youth worker, a refugee from Somalia, and a number of part-time youth workers and tutors employed directly by the borough. The full-time youth worker was interviewed.

The Project focuses much of its work on education, training and employment, through the following activities:

- Advice, information and guidance on education, employment and training. Counselling for young people and parents, summer schools, ESOL, and literacy classes in small groups as well as employment oriented courses;

- Support with job hunting skills, job applications, CVs, interview skills and personal references;
- Help with personal action plans and progression routes;
- Help with grant applications (mandatory, discretionary and others);
- Empower parents by raising their awareness about their children's adolescence period and how to cope with it; and
- Support and help in diverse needs across a range of non-educational activities.

(from Project publicity, 1999)

The Annual Report provides a detailed rationale for working closely with parents and families and local Somali community organisations.

The youth worker talked about how he approaches working in the community and with parents:

"The core of the work is in the relationships, in informal hard talking. Cross cultural shock leads to cultural conflict. I talk to parents. I share my own parenting experience. I explain that cross cultural shock is not their fault and that they should not blame the young people; that this is the issue that they must learn to deal with. I explain that they don't have to compare life with Somali life – that it's here and to see it from another angle. I challenge them to think critically about the old system, not to adhere to their systems in Somalia. This requires of me communication skills, listening, questioning and understanding – it's so easy to tell the problems, it's difficult to pose the solutions."

Initial approaches from the Project to the Youth Service for collaboration met with the response: *"Tell the young Somalis to use the services that we already provide"*. As project workers found that this approach did not work, they made contact with the local youth centre. Since this was not in use on Friday evenings, facilities were offered for a youth activity club for a three hour session. Activities include: recreation, leisure and informal programmes of social education and personal development through full participation in group activities and discussions or one-to-one, peer support and case work records. The club has a regular membership of about 30 young people, with average attendance of 20 per week, mainly boys. Football scores highly on the list of activities with trophies to show for its success. Work is underway to develop this aspect of the work, and especially to increase involvement of young women by engaging a female youth worker.

In 1997–98 the youth worker (a qualified engineer) was able to join the local

Youth Service's part-time youth workers' training course, offered through Brunel University. He gained the local qualification in 1998. Asked what he learned:

"It developed my professional approaches; it provided opportunities for me to articulate my practices within a theoretical and professional framework. It improved my confidence, my skills, and my creativity in making sense of my interactions with young people."

Undertaking his training with mainstream youth workers had advantages and disadvantages:

"It gave me contact with mainstream workers and created networks. It gave me knowledge and understanding of the system. It increased my personal confidence to gain work in the mainstream. But you see yourself as an outsider, totally different culture, language and experience. It led to 'cultural filtering' – because of my culture I had certain expectations of young people because of age, status, gender etc. For example, if I saw a young person smoking I would approach them and say 'This is not good for you.' That is not the case anymore. This is where I realised that we (as parents) need to develop second thoughts. My attitudes were challenged, I learned about the culture of young people here and I experienced what I call 'cross cultural shock'."

Interview Four: The Bede Youth Adventure Project

This is a project of the Bede House Association, a multi-purpose voluntary organisation in Bermondsey, London Borough of Southwark.

The Project's stated aims are:

- to enable young people to develop their potential through adventure activities, especially those who are often not encouraged to do so, such as young women, young people from Black and ethnic minority communities, young disabled people and young people from the inner city;
- to give young people opportunities to spend time together in an environment which helps them to learn to make decisions; develop rules which promote the wellbeing of others as well as themselves, and experience independence and autonomy;
- to enable young people to share new experiences and develop respectful relationships with each other and with adults; and

- to offer opportunities for young people to take risks and to experience success in activities which are challenging and which often feel dangerous (although they are actually safe), enabling them to discover and develop new skills and abilities and to strengthen their self confidence and belief in themselves.

The Project achieves these aims by working with young people in small groups, through detached youth work as well as on-site, and through regular day trips and residential experiences. It has three full-time youth workers and an extensive stock of equipment and networks to support the work through adventure activities.

For the first time, the Project has developed targeted work with young Somalis whose communities are growing in this part of London. Starting with a detached youth work programme, a youth club for young Somalis has been operating since the autumn of 1999. One full-time youth worker, a black woman, takes responsibility for the group and agreed to be interviewed.

The Project has been aware for some time of young Somalis living in the area, but had failed in the past to attract them. A detached youth work programme did not initially succeed in making meaningful contact. When a new worker was recruited in mid-1999, her job description focused on this need.

In her words:

"The first port of call was to make contact with Somali community leaders – to discuss the possibilities and needs. We contacted someone who was working with young Somali men in the Deptford area. I was able to meet with some of these young people (who were over 16 years) and discuss what they felt were the needs. Bede House Association had recently developed a relationship with the local Somali community who now run a Saturday School in the Bede community centre, so I met the leaders of the Saturday School. They were very supportive of the idea of developing youth work. Working with one of the Saturday School teachers, I organised a one week play-scheme for young Somali people during the summer holidays. The majority of the young people who participated live in the Bermondsey area and these were their first experiences of getting away. We took the 8 to 11-year-olds to ice-skating and to the zoo, and the 12 to 18-year-olds to the cinema and to Thorpe Park. From that we were able to establish the youth club on Thursday evenings."

A core group of ten young people attend the club of whom three are 12 to 15-year-old girls. Most but not all have lived here some time. All are bilingual. They've planned their own programme for their second term which includes: fencing, dry slope skiing, high-board diving, cooking and discussion groups on racism, bullying and violence in school.

> "When they were planning their programme this term, I asked them to fill in a short questionnaire on what they think their club is doing for them. They said they enjoy being with other young people doing all kinds of different activities, all of which are new to them. I think we may be offering a sort of supportive transition to this culture for them. I know they always arrive early for the club and when I asked them why they said it was good to get out of the house. They have got so much energy and I think the kinds of activities they do in their club gets some of it released."

Asked what issues arise in the work and how she addresses them, the worker continued:

> "For the young people racism is clearly a big issue, on the streets and in school. Last week we were driving past another local youth club and they started talking about how racist it was and how they had heard of two young black people being chased and threatened near there by a group of young white boys. At school there seems to be lots of fighting and they keep finding themselves in real situations."

> "As a black woman I tend to empathise a lot with them as young black people. They do not talk with me a great deal about their experiences in Somalia, or discuss the things their parents have been through. I tend to feel they may need _not_ to talk about these things and I do not push them. I do not pry, and I do not ask too many questions. I work with what they bring, and slowly they are opening up. I expect it to take time."

As a new area of work:

> "I keep thinking there may be a lot more I could be doing with them, and I'm not sure what, e.g. there's a young man who arrived very recently. He's told me that his father died in the war, that his mother is still in Africa, and that he lives with his brother. I keep wondering what else I could be doing with him. It takes a long time to make relationships. It is a very new area for me and I am learning all the time. I know I've got limitations too."

The worker said that much more work could be done and she expressed the desire to meet with other youth workers with experience of working with Somalis. She also thought it might be good to employ a Somali youth worker. She thought the young Somalis benefited from attending a mainstream youth project. The Project offered a different kind of environment in which they can meet other people, and learn new things. This way they get the best of two worlds.

Examples of Youth Work with Young Refugees: Findings:

- The curriculum for youth work is attractive to young refugees and will engage them. By its very nature it can be flexibly developed to address the specific needs of diverse groups of young refugees;
- Collaboration between mainstream and refugee community sectors is necessary. Mainstream support to refugee community organisations, in the form of access to a wide range of resources, advice and expertise on the job, and training to develop refugee youth workers is felt to be essential;
- Mainstream organisations benefit from working closely with RCOs to inform and support the development of their initiatives in working with young refugees;
- Refugee workers and workers in mainstream organisations want dialogue and mutual learning opportunities. Forums for encouraging and facilitating this need to be established;
- Qualified refugee youth workers are needed in both sectors to articulate the issues for young refugees, develop relevant and appropriate responses, and provide a conduit for refugee communities to statutory systems, networks and resources in the wider environment

Section Six:

MOVING FORWARD – DEVELOPING YOUTH WORK PROVISION IN REFUGEE COMMUNITIES

This section suggests essential elements for effective, appropriate and relevant youth work provision for refugee communities. These elements arise from the exploration of the diverse perspectives of young refugees and adults within their communities undertaken in this research.

Young refugees' perceptions of their needs (discussed in Section Two of this report) were primarily focused on the need for safety, friendship and a place to 'belong.' They expressed the need for time, space and resources for a range of activities to combat loneliness and boredom and provide opportunities to have fun with other young people, for competition, to get out and about, and opportunities to learn more about this country. They expressed needs for education, training and employment and access to advice and support to facilitate independence and integration.

Refugee adults' perceptions of the needs of young refugees (discussed in Section Three of the report) tended to focus more on the problematic issues arising in the lives of young refugees, their families and communities. Issues of 'torn cultural identity,' 'cross cultural shock,' 'inter-generational conflict' and 'double alienation' tended to be highlighted and articulated more by adults rather than young people.

In suggesting essential elements for a youth work curriculum, we need to explore how to balance these two sets of perceptions. We must meet young refugees' perceptions of their needs with a youth work approach through which refugee communities may effectively address some of the deeper issues (identified by refugee adults) for the whole community and beyond.

Furthermore, we need to remember that this research does not include the views from young refugees who are, at present, alienated from their communities and/or at risk or on the streets. In suggesting elements for youth work provision for young refugees, we have remained aware of this group, and seek to suggest measures which may prevent such alienation in the future.

Finally, while we take as our starting point the premise that refugee community organisations have a major part to play in developing youth work provision for young refugees (Section Three of report), it is evident that the work is unlikely to develop beyond its current limitations without the support of mainstream youth services and funders.

Elements for Effective, Relevant, and Appropriate Youth Work Provision in Refugee Communities

Earlier in this report we suggest four characteristics for an effective youth work curriculum (pages 9 and 10). In this section we take each of these four, inter-related characteristics and discuss how, in combination, they may be utilised to suggest essential, appropriate and relevant elements of a youth work provision for refugee communities.

1. "An Experiential Curriculum"

Youth work starts with the perceived needs of young people themselves. As we have seen, young refugees, like all young people, do not want to be bored or isolated. As for all young people, programmes of activity for young refugees, which will expand horizons and develop potential, need to be varied, supportive and challenging:

- cultural activities, celebrations and discussions can assist young refugees not only to gain knowledge of their culture, but to critically reflect on it, and subsequently develop it;
- advice, information and referral services are essential, integral elements of this experiential curriculum with emphasis on assisting young refugees, over time, to learn to undertake these activities for themselves and for each other;
- art, drama, and music can be important vehicles for expression and problem solving for young refugees who may have experienced trauma and/or who may need assistance to develop their sense of identity in ambivalent cross cultural contexts;
- sport can release emotional energy, promote physical and mental health, generate teamwork, provide a sense of achievement and improved self confidence, and opportunities to engage with the wider environment through competition;
- outdoor pursuits can provide adventure, risk (through activity which is

actually safe) and inter-dependence as well as opportunities to travel and explore this country;

- computers can facilitate useful learning opportunities and communications across the world;
- opportunities to explore issues like cultural history, sex education and sexuality, bullying and violence, sexism and racism, drugs, homelessness and wider community issues in a safe, culturally sensitive and non-judgmental environment could support young refugees in negotiating peer pressure and other pressures to conform, and in developing positive identity for self and the community at large;
- accreditation programmes through, for example, the Duke of Edinburgh Award, or the Youth Achievement Award can promote self esteem as well as provide concrete evidence of achievements, positive attitudes and skills to the outside world; and
- cooking and eating together can support social development as well as provide a necessary basis on which to proceed with everything else!

An important element of this experiential curriculum is active encouragement and support for young people to form meaningful and supportive relationships with their peers through the medium of doing things together, reflecting on their experiences and generating ideas and plans for further activity.

2. "Participation in Decision Making"

Young refugees are the community leaders of the future. Developing youth work programmes *with* young refugees rather than *for* them can promote relationships, build effective groups, generate self confidence and self esteem and promote young leaders.

Effective participation in their own affairs may counter-balance the overwhelming burden of responsibility often generated in young refugees within their family (as discussed by RCO coordinators in Section Three of this report).

Evidence from the research suggests that, initially, many young refugees need assistance to access the most mainstream of activities: swimming pools, cinemas, ice rinks. Participating in decision making and the organisation of their own programmes can develop interpersonal skills and broaden knowledge of the wider community and the possibilities available.

3. "Voluntaryism"

A critical question for RCO coordinators was: "Do they come because they want to or because their parents impel them?" Evidence from the young refugees suggests that an attractive and relevant programme developed from the young refugees' perceived needs will attract them. Assurances of confidentiality and a non-judgmental attitude are likely to generate safety and trust. Acceptance and acknowledgment of the issues that they perceive to be important may ultimately motivate their involvement in the wider life of the community.

4. "Non-directive Relationships Between Adults and Young People"

Many young refugees perceived their relationships with adults in terms of formal authority (they talked of teachers, immigration officers, police, social workers, and of course parents). Adults talked of young people mainly in problematic terms. Both young people and adults stressed the need for young refugees to experience acceptance, belonging, and a supportive, listening ear. If youth work provision in refugee communities is to be effective it requires adults who care, who can communicate, who are prepared to advocate, and who are able to skillfully negotiate the tensions and difficulties generated by inter-generational conflict.

Positive role models are essential and many young adult refugees could fill this role for their younger counterparts. Those who have themselves negotiated their way through some of the issues generated by 'cross cultural shock' and 'torn cultural identity' (Section Three of this report) and have first hand experience of the 'day-time/night-time culture,' could be instrumental in assisting young people towards developing self esteem and self determining yet responsible attitudes. These adults may need support and assistance themselves to deal with the complex emotional and dynamic relationships implied here through youth work training and ongoing professional supervision.

It should not be forgotten that most refugee communities contain a wealth of talent and skills across many of the suggested curriculum areas. These people can be a significant resource to young people and provide further important role models.

In addition to the above, we suggest four further elements for effective youth work provision in refugee communities: the need for an individual support, advice and information service; the need for partnerships with the wider environment of community and youth services; the need for reasonable levels of resources to make possible suggested programmes; and the need for parallel services to support the 'special needs' of young refugees and their families.

5. Resources

Evidence from this research suggests that most refugee community organisations are severely under-resourced for this work. Refugee families are, more often than not, functioning at or below poverty levels. Young refugees in hostels have virtually no financial resources. In the main, the youth work curriculum for refugee communities requires 100 per cent resourcing.

Funding sources are urgently required not just to provide staffing but to provide full support to the curriculum: for equipment, travel costs, entry fees, food, room hire, residential costs, and materials, e.g. for art and craft, drama productions and music.

6. Partnerships and Other Links with the Mainstream Community

Linked with the resource element, partnership would seem essential to effective provision. Local authority Youth Services and the large voluntary youth work organisations have significant and varied resources (including expertise) which can be made available to refugee organisations. Partnership implies a two way relationship; therefore the findings of this research as to the lack of engagement of mainstream organisations with young refugees and RCOs must be reversed.

As has been seen, young refugees living with their families straddle two cultures and for many this can literally result in what has been termed a 'day-time/night-time culture.' Any strategy for working with young refugees will need to acknowledge and work with these cross cultural dynamics, and an effective and relevant curriculum will provide opportunities for young refugees to mix with their peers in the wider community in a safe and creative environment, e.g. by inviting school friends to join in community celebrations and young people's events within the community organisation.

Similarly, young unaccompanied refugees expressed the need not only for secure contact with their own community, but for assistance in accessing the wider community with the goal of integration. This would imply the creation of 'bridges' to the wider community, e.g. cross cultural events, competitions and a broad range of social activities undertaken in partnership with other youth organisations.

Finally many RCOs expressed urgent needs to learn the principles and practices of youth work. As qualified youth workers are scarce on the ground in refugee communities, consideration could usefully be given to how mainstream Youth Services could actively support refugee communities to learn 'on-the-job.' This could be done, for example by secondment of staff, representation on youth work steering groups, and inclusion of refugee communities in the broader scope of borough Youth Service activities, including training.

7. The Need for Parallel Approaches

Finally, this research provides evidence of the need for a broad range of other dedicated services for young refugees and their families. These are critical if youth work provision is to be prioritised or effective:

- *Supplementary education and mother tongue classes*

  Many RCOs offer supplementary schooling operating on a shoestring for large numbers of young people. Supplementary schooling clearly provides essential input for young people struggling to catch up with their peers in mainstream schools, and mother tongue classes not only support cultural development but aid and assist overall language skills, promoting all round achievement.

  Given the large numbers of young refugees attending supplementary schooling it is clear that it can provide an essential jumping-off point for developing youth work provision in refugee communities, providing ongoing support to young people as they grow out of the supplementary school. As such, supplementary schooling requires a much more adequate resource and support base.

- *Counselling and school support services*

  Young refugees' experiences of schooling are widely discussed in this report. Many recently arrived young people need extensive support for integration into mainstream schooling for many reasons. These include interruptions to their previous schooling, the need to learn the language and the systems, and the frequently negative reactions of adults and peers which can lead to bullying, aggression, truancy and exclusion.

  Coordinated approaches to supporting young refugees in schools are essential. Collaboration between schools and RCOs has been suggested. For example, mainstream teachers could become formally involved in supplementary schools, and/or RCOs could be formally encouraged to develop school liaison provision in partnership with key school professionals.

- *Work with parents*

  Many refugee adults talked of the need for extensive work to support parents in their relationships with their young people and in the negotiations which arise through inter-generational conflict and 'cross cultural shock.' Parents themselves are often at a loss, for example, around issues of sex education, how to recognise drug abuse, or the implications within this society of approaches to punishing children (e.g. the implications of the Children Act and the UN Convention on the Rights of the Child). RCOs are suggested as being best placed to generate the kinds of dialogue and learning opportunities which may assist parents.

Section Seven:

MOVING FORWARD – RECOMMENDATIONS FOR POLICY AND PRACTICE

Our Overarching Recommendation is the Development of an Appropriate and Relevant Youth Work Provision for Refugee Communities

We offer a starting point for dialogue in the previous section (Section Six – Moving Forward, Developing Youth Work Provision in Refugee Communities).

We have suggested to the Barbara Melunsky Fund and its partner organisations that they facilitate this dialogue in all ways possible.

We ask all main providers of Youth Services to participate in this dialogue with refugees, refugee community organisations and other refugee agencies.

We see the participation of the following agencies as essential:

- local authority youth services
- voluntary youth agencies (local and national)
- providers of youth work training (full and part-time)
- the National Youth Agency
- the Department for Education and Employment (DfEE)
- the Home Office
- major funding agencies
- refugee community organisations
- other refugee agencies
- Refugee Council

The following specific recommendations are offered to encourage and assist this dialogue:

Recommendations Directed to Local Authority Youth Services and to Other Main Providers of Youth Services.

All Youth Services (however organised) should consult with local people knowledge-able about the needs of young refugees in the area under consideration, possibly forming an advisory committee (such as a committee to include refugees and/or the children of refugees).

Grants to refugee community organisations wishing to provide services for young people should be favourably considered. RCOs should be encouraged to apply for funding and support should be given to assist organisations to deal with the paperwork.

Youth work with young refugees requires high levels of funding, including 100 per cent grants.

Existing providers of Youth Services should be encouraged to provide facilities for young refugees. This may include:

a) The use of premises, especially at times not already being used.

b) The support and supervision of staff already in post, by specially recruited staff, or in cooperation with a local refugee organisation.

c) The use of sports, arts, drama, music, crafts and computing facilities and equipment by young refugees with staffing by one or a combination of the above methods.

d) **As a matter of urgency,** make available the use of convenient premises for young refugees, particularly for those living in hostels and hotels, so that they may meet for tea/coffee, light refreshment, etc. with some activities to occupy their time and overcome problems of boredom and loneliness.

e) The provision of ongoing advice and support to RCOs.

f) None of the above recommendations in this section is intended to exclude efforts to encourage young refugees to use existing mainstream provision when it is open to all. One of the outcomes of the other recommendations in this section may be an increased use of mainstream provision by young refugees, especially if they gain confidence with workers and in their local communities. This will be enhanced by consultation and collaboration with local refugee communities to ensure relevant and appropriate provision.

Supplementary schools can provide a firm basis for developing youth work with young refugees. Currently many of these schools are operated by volunteers in RCOs with inadequate resources and with very large numbers of children. Local authority

Youth Services should seek to enable the provision of higher levels of resourcing and support for the development of supplementary schools in RCOs.

Youth Service providers should attempt to widen their recruitment policies to include people of refugee origin who speak the languages and understand the culture of young refugees. These people should be considered as full-time, part-time and voluntary workers.

Providers should also encourage people of refugee origin to undertake part-time and full-time training to work with young refugees.

Providers should encourage current full-time, part-time and voluntary workers to undertake training to better equip them to work with young refugees.

Providers should encourage current full-time, part-time and voluntary workers to undertake training to equip them to work positively with non-refugee young people to raise the young people's understanding of the issues and to work for greater social inclusion.

Recommendations Addressed to Providers of Youth Work Training for Full-time Professional Qualifications and Qualified Part-time Work

To recruit an increased number of workers of refugee origin.

To develop training courses to provide non-refugee workers with the skills needed to work more effectively with young refugees.

To develop courses that can provide appropriate support for participants of refugee origin.

To develop elements of the core curriculum to incorporate key issues relating to young refugees and refugee communities.

To develop elements of the core curriculum to assist youth work trainees to develop a broad analysis of the refugee issue, locally, nationally and internationally. To assist them in their work with non-refugees.

Recommendations to the National Youth Agency and National Voluntary Youth Organisations

To collect all information relevant to developing youth work with young refugees and to disseminate this information, through their publications and other materials.

To encourage and assist all providers of youth services to work with young refugees.

To lobby government (central and local) and all other providers of resources to develop adequate services for young refugees.

To encourage such research on youth work and young refugees as seems necessary. In light of dispersal, formalised by the 1999 Immigration and Asylum Act, further research on the national youth work picture is now urgently needed.

Recommendations to the Department for Education and Employment (DfEE)

To issue such circulars and advice as necessary to establish that work with young refugees is a priority for the Youth Service.

To act as the coordinator for central government departments (primarily the Home Office, Health and Social Services and DETR) on policies for young refugees.

To liaise with the Refugee Council and other bodies, especially bodies representing refugee communities in the UK in order to assess and promote the needs of young refugees.

Recommendations to the Home Office

That the position of newly arrived refugees be clarified to allow them to work voluntarily without endangering their application for asylum. Specifically, that a dispensation be given to asylum seekers who do not have permission to have paid work to act as voluntary workers for registered charities or for a public service such as a local authority. Such voluntary workers should be entitled to receive travel expenses and standard expenses as allowed to all volunteer workers.

As 30 to 40 per cent of current asylum seekers will be granted refugee status or exceptional leave to remain (on current figures), any provision for asylum seekers must consider issues of settlement and future full participation in civil society.

Re: Funding and support arrangements in the Immigration and Asylum Act, in addition to the Home Office funding accommodation and basic living costs of new asylum seekers as detailed in the Act, we recommend that funding be available for other services including Youth Services. In considering the financial burden on local authorities, services for young refugees and especially for Youth Services should be considered.

Recommendations to the BMF and other Funders

To continue to monitor the situation with relation to young refugees.

To conduct research to discover the gaps in services provided by statutory and professional bodies.

To actively involve refugee workers in future research programmes of this kind. These need to be diverse in terms of origin and gender and capable of making contact with young people in informal settings. Formal, accredited research training could enhance such programmes and build the capacity of refugee communities to actively research their own issues.

To use the findings of this research and of the earlier youth work training programme to inform, promote and support training for the vast range of volunteers and part-time workers in refugee community organisations whose needs have been clearly shown in this research.

In the first instance a series of shorter, introductory courses would be of value – to encourage some of the many people involved in working with young people to critically explore their own roles and functions. These shorter courses (perhaps of three or four days) could then feed into in depth accredited training programmes. BMF may wish to consider taking the lead on the establishment of a full programme leading to a national community and youth work professional qualification, perhaps utilising an apprenticeship model.

To continue to raise the visibility of issues concerning the development of youth work for young refugees.

REFERENCES

Short bibliography of references informing the preparation of this report:

- Active Community Unit (Home Office), (1999) *Community Self-Help*, Report of Policy Action Team 9, ACU, Home Office
- Aden, M. (1996) *Somali Refugee Youth Development Project: Annual Report*, Acton, London
- *Armenian Voice*, the newsletter for the London Armenian Community, (Winter 2000) published by the Centre for Armenian Information and Advice, London
- Asylum Rights Campaign, (1999) *Out of Sight, Out of Mind, a Report on the Dispersal of Asylum Seekers in the UK*, ARC, London
- Ayotte W. (1998) *Supporting Unaccompanied Children in the Asylum Process*, Save the Children, London
- Berhane, T. (1998) *The Involvement of Young Refugees in the Lambeth Young Refugees Development Project*, unpublished
- Brewin M. and Demetriades A. (1998) *Raising the Profile of Invisible Students, Practical and Peer Led Approaches to Enhancing Educational and Emotional Support for Refugee and Asylum Seeking Children in Schools*, Children of the Storm, London
- British Red Cross, (1995/98) *Moving Stories, A Young Person's Guide to Refugees in Today's World*, Youthplus, A Red Cross Youth Publication
- Dept. for Education and Science, (1982) *Experience and Participation, Report of the Review Group on the Youth Service in England. Cmnd 8686.* HMSO, London
- DfEE, (2000) *Connexions: The Best Start in Life for Every Young Person*, DfEE publications
- DfEE, (1999) *Jobs for All*, Report of Policy Action Team 1, DfEE publications
- Evelyn Oldfield Unit, *Annual Reports and Various Reports of Work*, available

from the Evelyn Oldfield Unit, LVSRC, 356 Holloway Road, London N7 6PA

- Home Office, (1999) *A Consultation Paper on the Integration of Recognised Refugees in the UK*, Immigration & Nationality Division, Croydon

- Horn of Africa Youth Scheme, (1998) *"Let's Spell it Out"* HAYS with Save the Children, London

- McAfee, B. (1998*) "... instead of medicine,"* Refugee Action

- Refugee Council, (1999), *Refugee Resources in the UK, 1999*, Refugee Council

- Refugee Council, *Inexile The Refugee Council Magazine*, (published bi-monthly), London

- Richman, N. (1996*) 'They Don't Recognise Our Dignity,' a Study of the Psycho-Social Needs of Refugee Children and Families in Hackney*, City and Hackney Community Services NHS Trust, Child and Adolescent Services

- Social Exclusion Unit, (2000a) *National Strategy for Neighbourhood Renewal: a Framework for Consultation,* Social Exclusion Unit, London

- Social Exclusion Unit, (2000b) *Policy Action Team Report Summaries: a Compendium*, Social Exclusion Unit, London [Note: this publication contains details of the 18 Policy Action Team reports – all obtainable from central government departments as listed on page 6 of the compendium]

- Social Exclusion Unit, (2000c) *Minority Ethnic Issues in Social Exclusion and Neighbourhood Renewal*, Social Exclusion Unit, London

- Wolde-Giyorgis, E. H., Kidane, S. and Ghelle, A. (1998) *Giving Refugee Children a Voice: Refugee Children and Young People's Experiences of Local Services*, Camden Family Service Unit, London

- Young People's Anti Poverty Project [YAPP], (1999) *Voices of Refugee Youth: the Views of Young Refugees in the London Borough of Greenwich,* YAPP, 12th Floor, Riverside House, Woolwich High Street, London SE18 6DN